# How to *Weave* Authentic Hawaiian Lauhala Bracelets

## A STEP-BY-STEP GUIDE

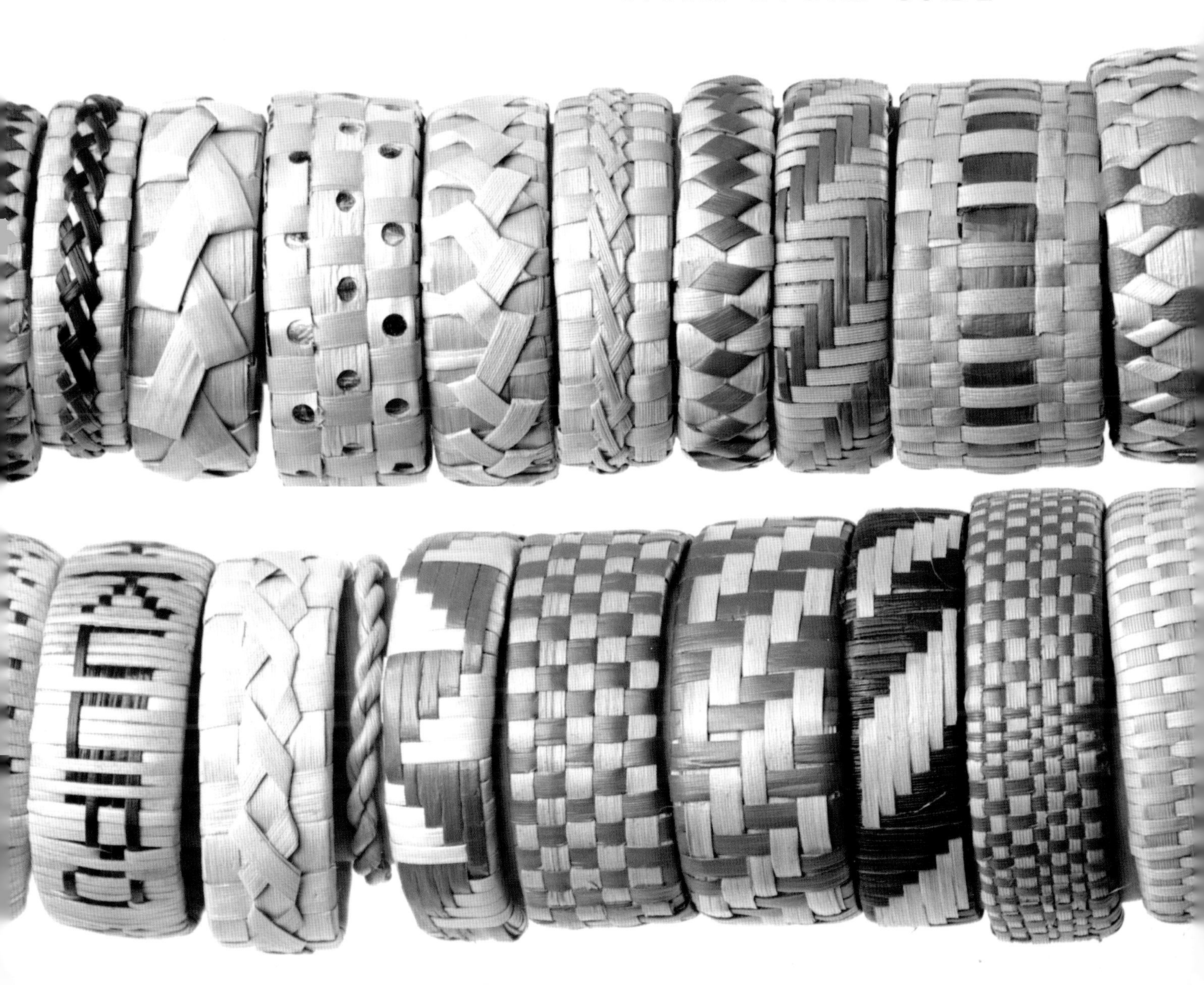

# How to *Weave* Authentic Hawaiian Lauhala Bracelets

**A STEP-BY-STEP GUIDE**

by **Jim Widess**

The Fourth Book in his series of
Traditional Hawaiian Crafts

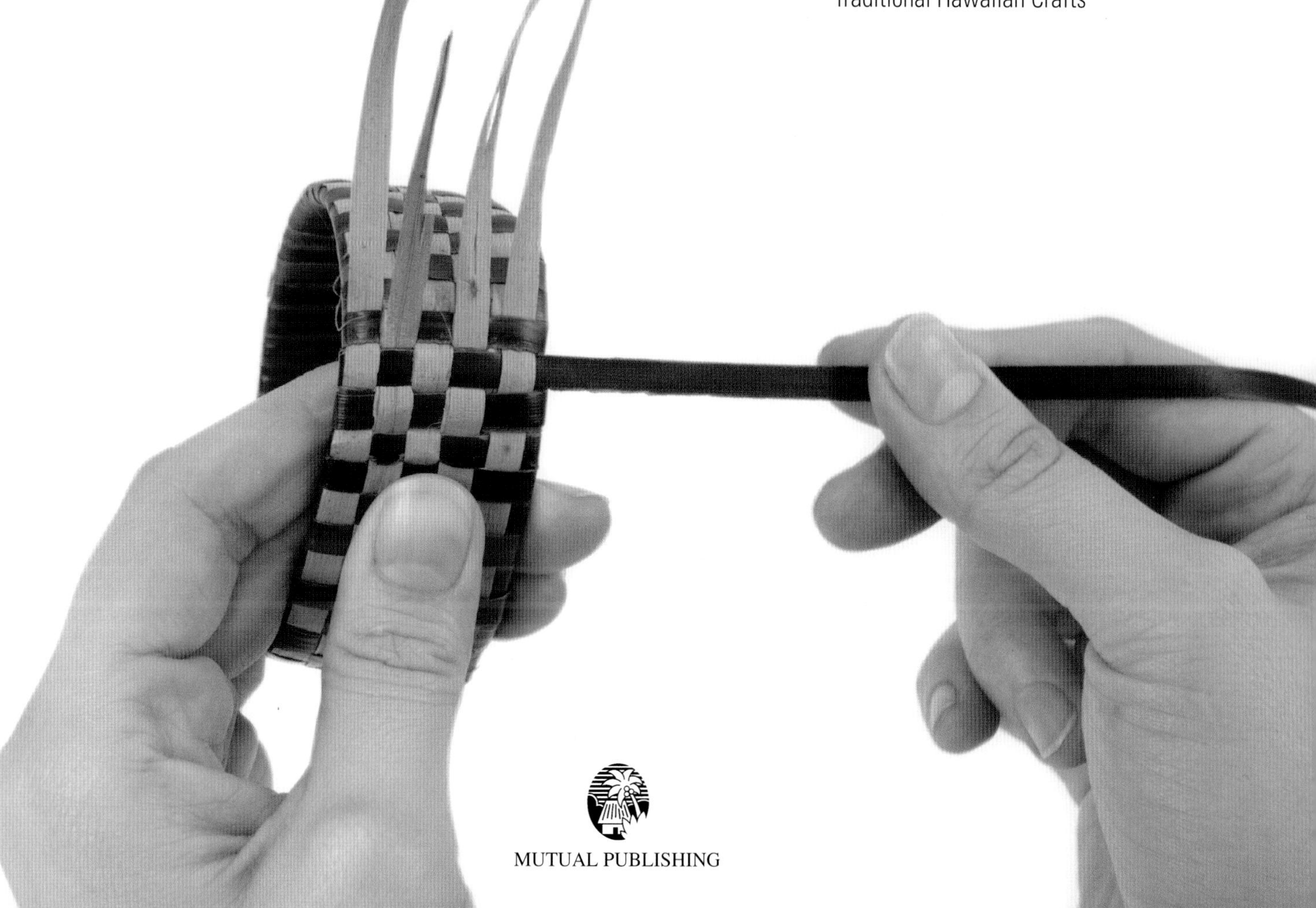

MUTUAL PUBLISHING

Library of Congress Cataloging-in-Publication Data

Widess, Jim.

How to weave authentic Hawaiian lauhala bracelets : a step-by-step guide / by Jim Widess.

p. cm.

Includes bibliographical references.

ISBN 1-56647-935-5 (softcover : alk. paper)

1. Lauhala weaving. 2. Bracelets. I. Title.

TT877.5.W53 2011

746.1'4--dc22

2011009677

First Printing, May 2011

Second Printing, July 2013

Third Printing, August 2015

Fourth Printing, April 2018

ISBN-10: 1-56647-935-5

ISBN-13: 978-1-56647-935-6

Design by Mardee Melton

Mutual Publishing, LLC

1215 Center Street, Suite 210

Honolulu, Hawai'i 96816

Ph: (808) 732-1709

Fax: (808) 734-4094

e-mail: info@mutualpublishing.com

www.mutualpublishing.com

Printed in South Korea

# Table of Contents

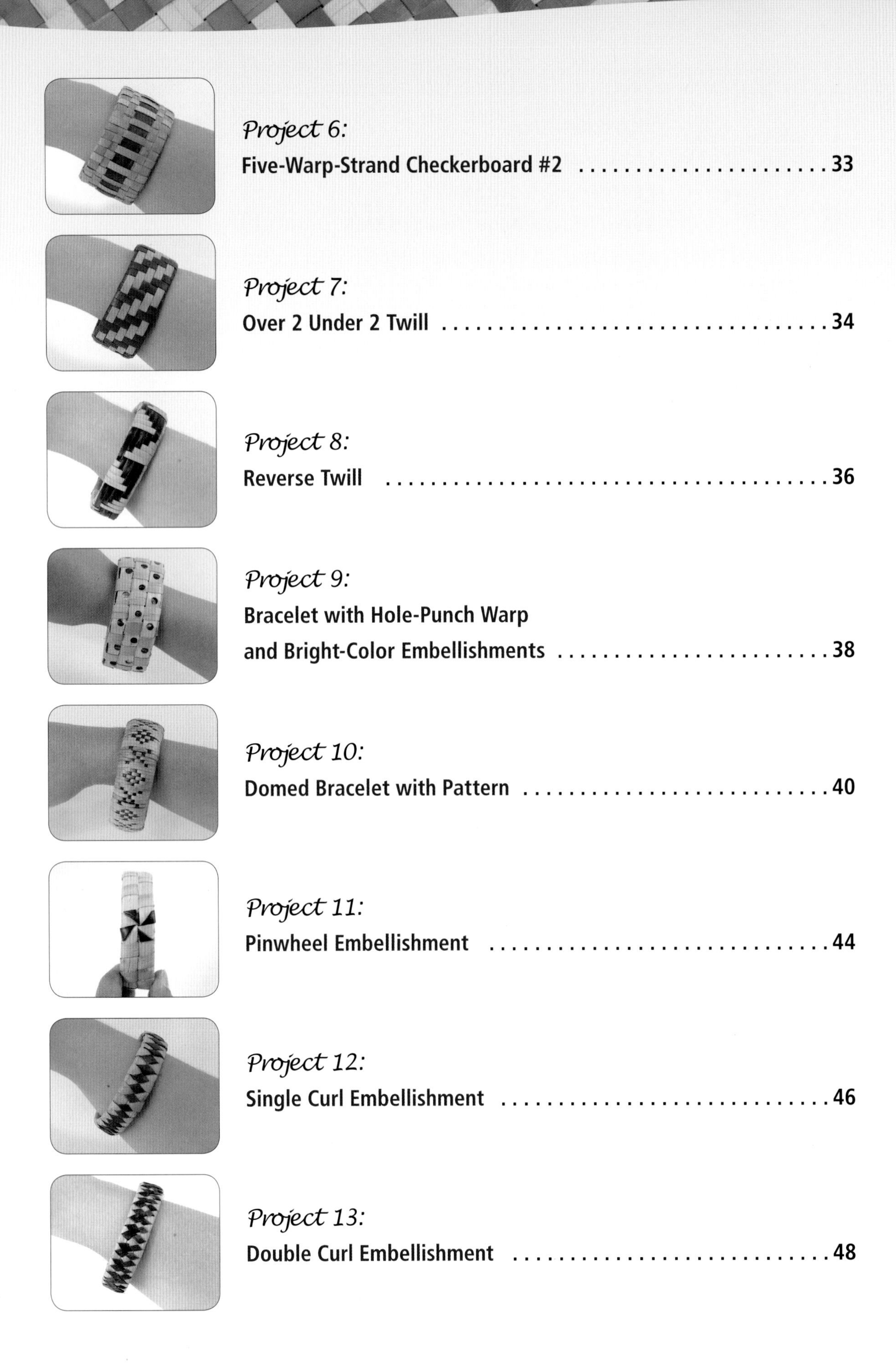

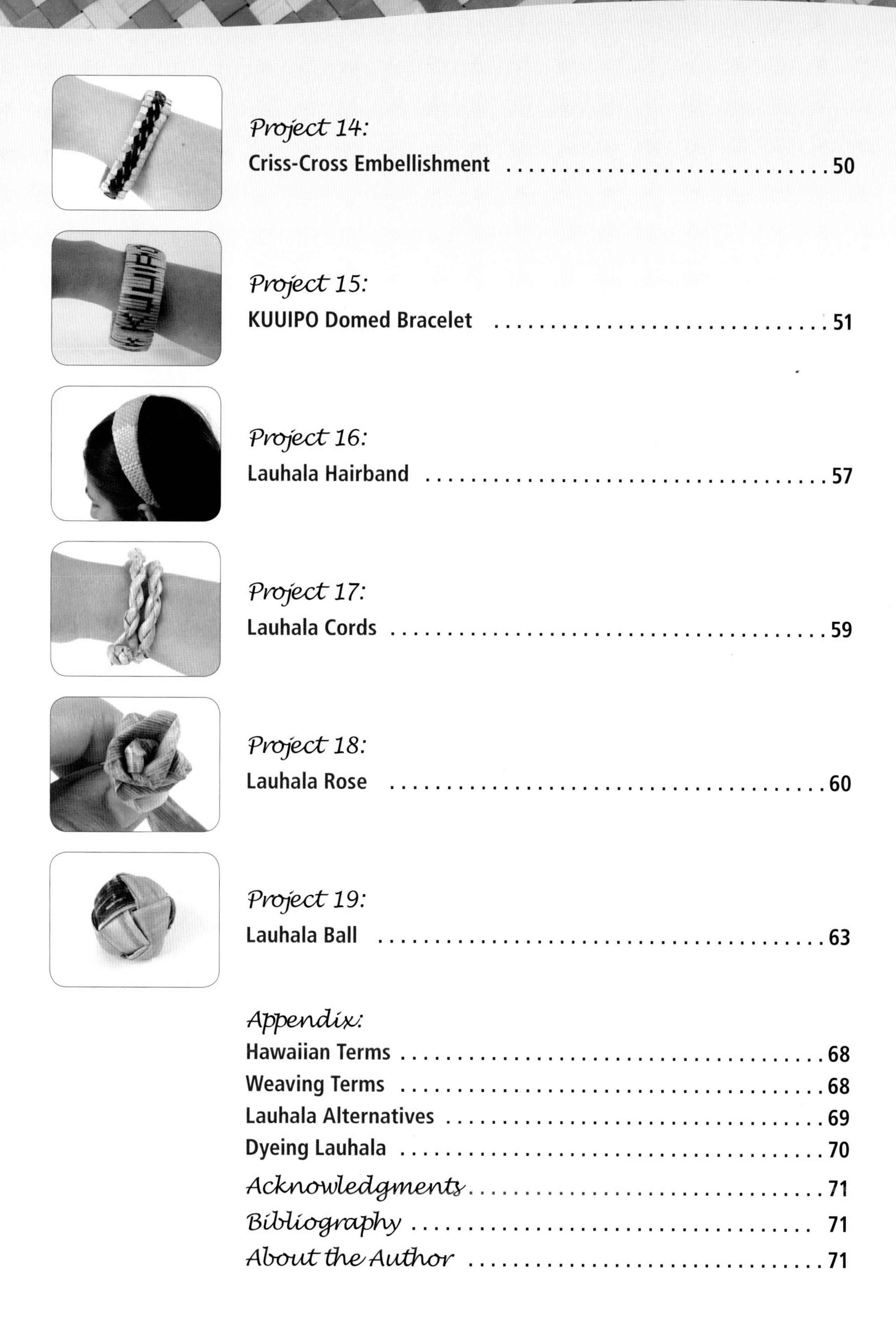

# Introduction

Probably the most important plant to the lives of the Hawaiian people is the hala tree. Known by its scientific genus, *Pandanus*, the hala tree provided food, medicine, and weaving materials. The weaving materials, stripped from the hala leaves (*lauhala*), were used for weaving sleeping mats, storage baskets, fans and adornments, and most importantly, the sails for the outrigger canoes that allowed the Polynesians to explore the South Pacific and discover the islands of Hawai'i.

*Lauhala* is an extremely strong fiber that retains its flexibility and softness for many years. This quality, plus its extraordinary length—up to 6.6 feet long and over 4 inches wide—and its availability throughout the South Pacific has made it the most desirable weaving element. This wonderful leaf of the *Pandanus* genus also has a thick waxy cuticle on the outside of the leaf,

*Hawaiian Canoe* by James Webber, artist on Captain Cook's expedition.

*A Canoe of the Sandwich Islands, the Rowers Masked* by John Webber, London, 1790.

Photo: Colleen Ricci

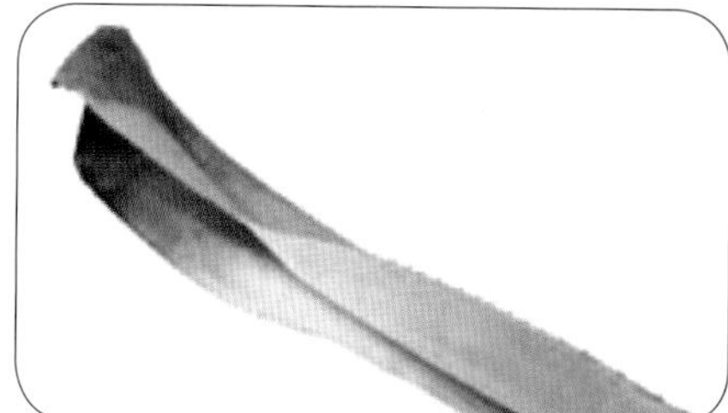

*Butt end of leaf showing thorny midrib.*

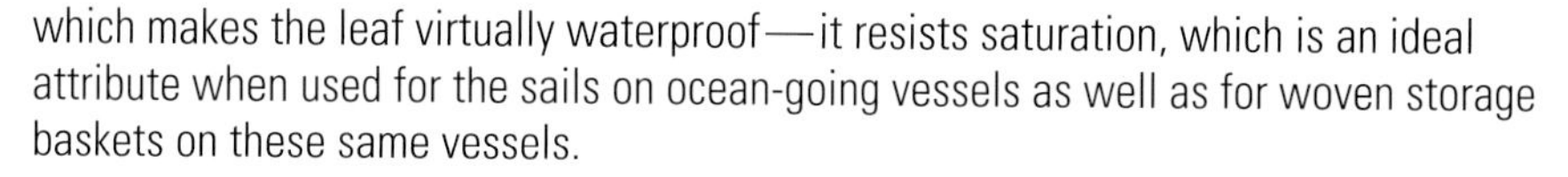

which makes the leaf virtually waterproof—it resists saturation, which is an ideal attribute when used for the sails on ocean-going vessels as well as for woven storage baskets on these same vessels.

The leaf is composed of straight, parallel, longitudinal veins, which easily strip into long, parallel-edged weaving elements for any chosen width—1/16 inch to 4 inches wide. Most species of the genus *Pandanus* have leaf borders that are finely toothed with sharp spines as well as a spiny-toothed midrib on the underside of the leaf. A few species are without these spines—notably a variegated (multi-colored) green and yellow leaf variety, which is commonly found on hotel grounds.

Photo: Sherri Carden

*Spineless, variegated variety.*

In the countries of Samoa, Tonga, and Fiji, *fala* leaves are picked green, soaked in the ocean for several days, and then laid out in the sun to dry. When it rains the leaves are quickly gathered and brought inside, and brought back out to the grass to dry when the shower stops. The green leaves will bleach white in a few days with this treatment. The seawater toughens the fiber.

For weaving hats, fans, and fine adornments, the fibrous underside of the leaf is scraped away from the thicker cuticle of the upper side of the green leaf. A sturdy seashell, the *'opihi*, is used as the scraper. The strong cuticle that is left is bleached white by the sun and sometimes dyed, using naturally occurring dyestuff, if color is required.

Photo: Lynn Tyrell

*Green lauhala on lava rock beach in Western Samoa.*

A simple, yet satisfying introduction to the weaving of *Pandanus* is the crafting of a *lauhala* bracelet. This project can be completed in an hour or two, and the pleasure of turning a found leaf into a beautiful woven object of adornment cannot be described. The multitude of patterns that are woven into the bracelet becomes an exciting, multi-cultural exercise, as these patterns are traditional to many peoples outside the South Pacific.

In most parts of the world, basket weaving has been an important aspect of the culture. People have depended on woven baskets for lightweight storage and transportation for over 10,000 years. Knowledge of the plants and their preparation has been passed down through generations of basket weavers.

And now this knowledge is being passed down to you.

**Some examples of traditional Hawaiian and Polynesian crafts.**

# Making a Safe Lauhala Stripper

## Traditional *Lauhala* Strippers

Collection of Donna Cockett

The photos above show a traditional *lauhala* stripping box built from koa wood. Removable 1/16-inch and 1/8-inch shims separate very sharp #11 hobby knife blades. A professional tool, its construction and use are beyond the scope of this book.

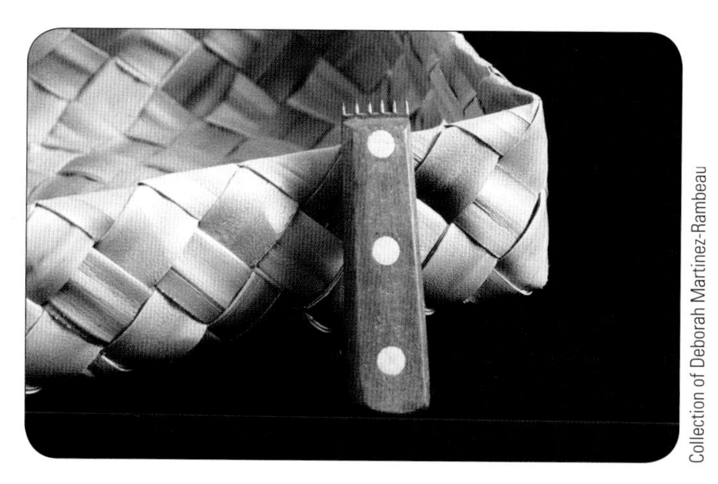

Collection of Deborah Martinez-Rambeau

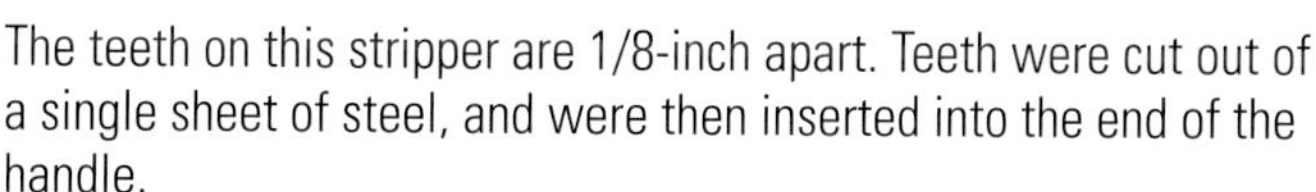

The teeth on this stripper are 1/8-inch apart. Teeth were cut out of a single sheet of steel, and were then inserted into the end of the handle.

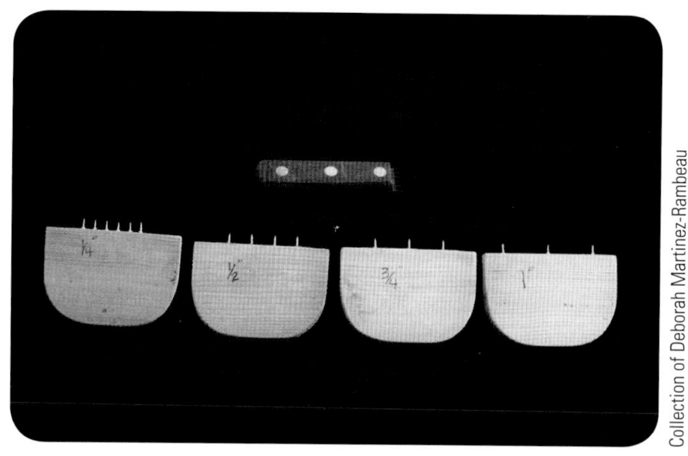

Collection of Deborah Martinez-Rambeau

This set of 4 strippers has increments of 1/4 inch, 1/2 inch, 3/4 inch, and 1 inch. They were made by driving 20-gauge wire nails into the end of a block of wood then cutting off the heads and sharpening the remaining shaft.

These are all dangerous tools, and we've got a safe alternative that any responsible child or young adult can make.

After studying the individual *lauhala* strippers above, I created the child-safe *lauhala* stripper on the following page from easily found craft supplies.

## Making a *Lauhala* Stripper That Is Safe for Children

**WHAT YOU'LL NEED:**

- Foamies™ sheets or door hangers, 6mm thick (approximately 1/4 inch) made by Darice. Available at most craft stores. You can substitute Pink Pearl™ or similar erasers for the Foamies™ if necessary.
- pencil
- 6-inch ruler or straight edge
- graph paper 8 squares to the inch and double-sided tape
- awl or ice pick
- dressmaker straight pins (1-1/4 inches long)
- white glue, superglue
- clothespins, binder clamps or similar clamps

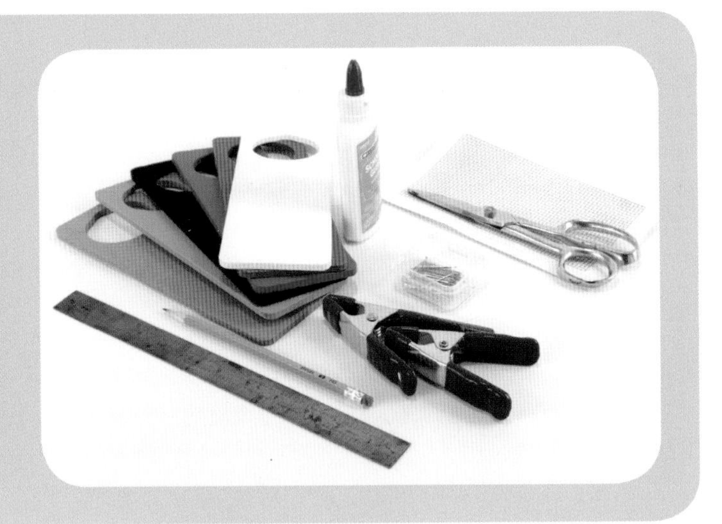

**1.** Cut two rectangles, 1-inch x 3-inches, from the 6mm (1/4 inch) sheet of Foamies™. These will be the stripper handles.

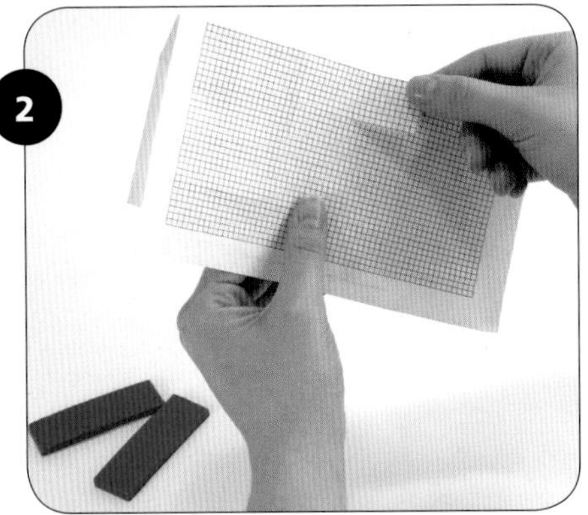

**2.** Peel one rectangle from a sheet of sticky-back mailing labels on which you have printed 8 squares per inch graph paper.

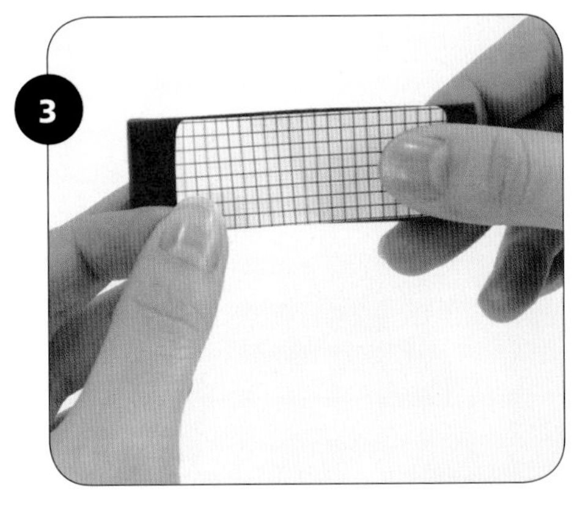

**3.** Carefully align the graph paper on top of one of the stripper handles so that the graph paper grid is parallel to the edges of the stripper handle.

**4.** With your pencil and the ruler, highlight every fourth short line on the graph paper—so that the space between your pencil lines is 1/2 inch.

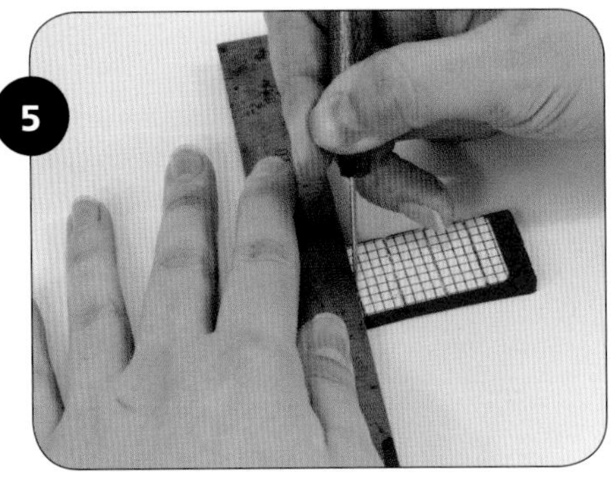

**5.** Using the ruler as a guide, go over your pencil lines with the point of the awl or ice pick so that the point of the awl cuts through the graph paper and also makes a shallow cut in the stripper handle.

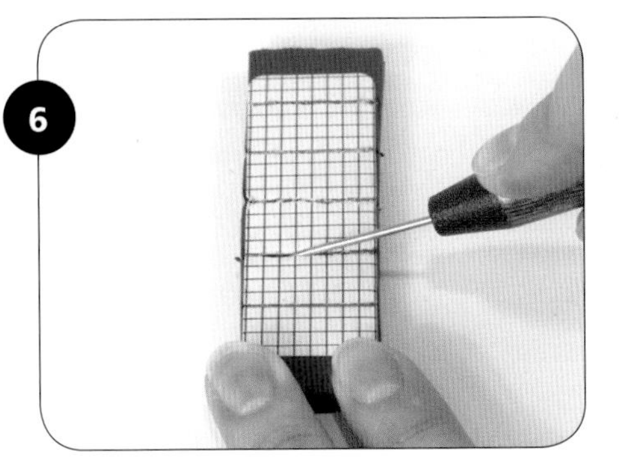

**6.** Using the ruler or straight edge and the awl, deepen the cut lines in the stripper handle until the cut is approximately 1/16 inch deep. You want the cut to be only as deep as the diameter of the dress pin shaft.

**7.** Lay 5 dress pins into the 5 cuts in the middle of the stripper handle.

**8.** If you slightly bend the stripper handle backwards you'll open the cuts and the pins will lay in easier.

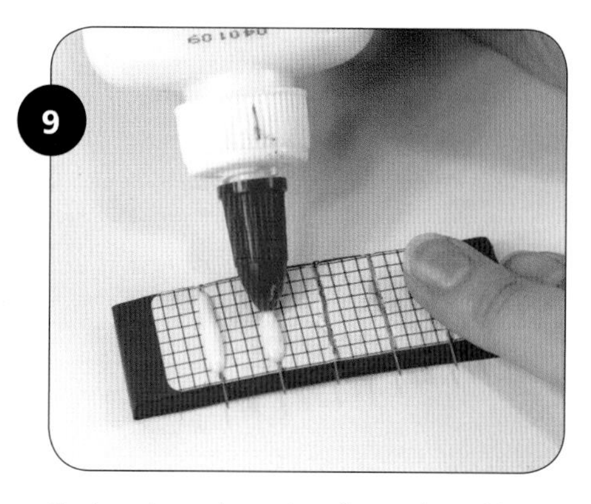

**9.** Lay the stripper handle on the table with the 5 dress pins in place and drizzle a little glue along each pin.

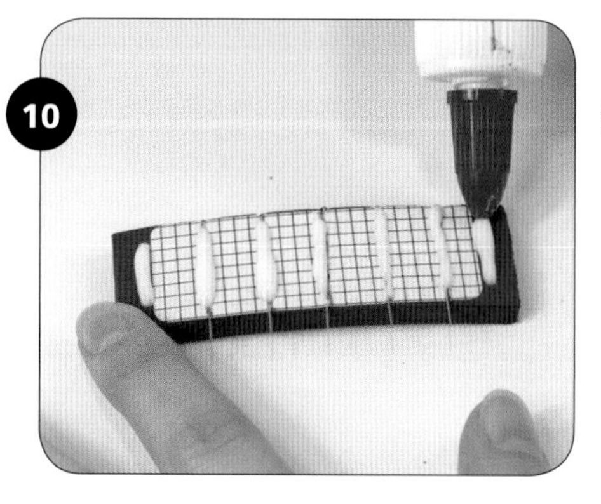

**10.** Then onto the rest of the stripper handle.

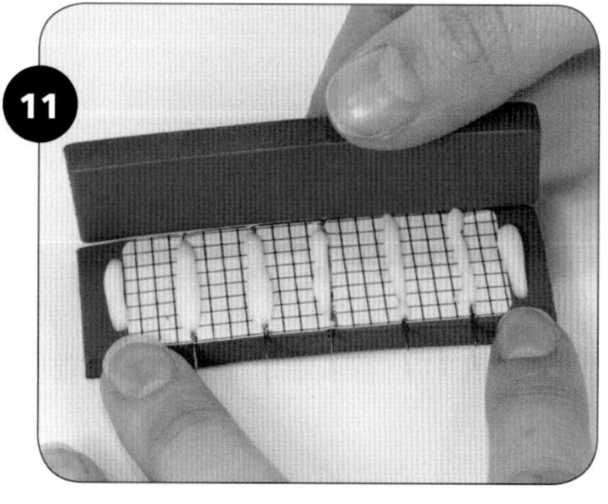

**11.** Pick up the second stripper handle and align it over the first stripper handle.

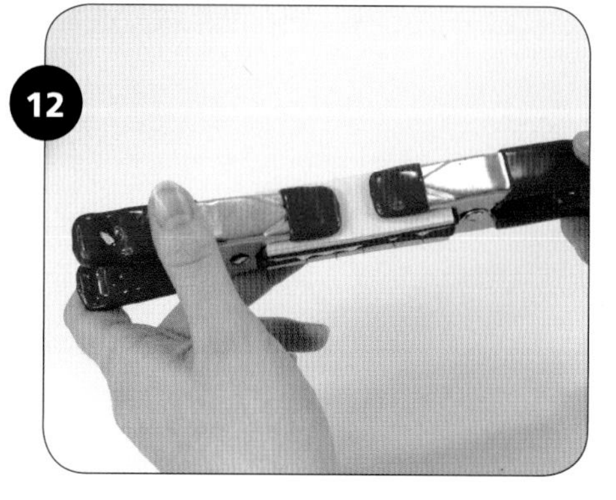

**12.** Clamp the two stripper handles together, making sure the pins stay in their cuts and the heads of the pins are pushed against the top of the stripper handle. We used two small pieces of wood or plastic between the clamps and the Foamies™ pieces. Allow the glue to set overnight.

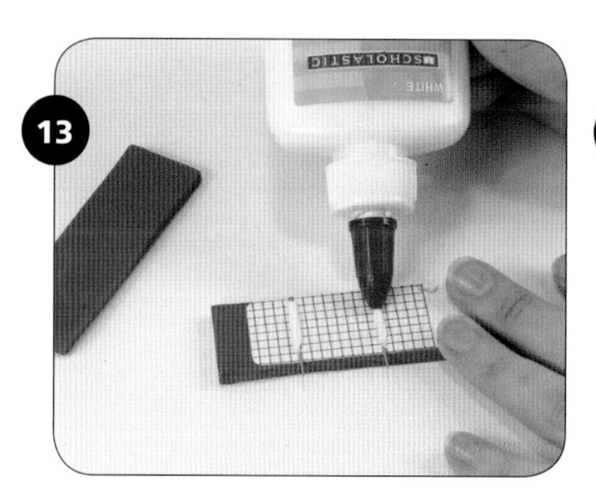

**13.** While you're waiting for the glue to dry, make a stripper handle with 2 pins, 8 squares apart (1 inch), which we'll use to make the bracelet foundation.

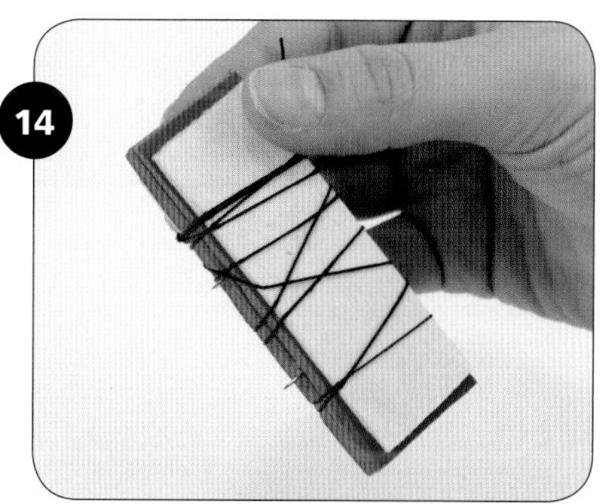

**14.** If you don't have any clamps, you can use a length of cord wrapped around the stripper handles to keep it together until the glue dries.

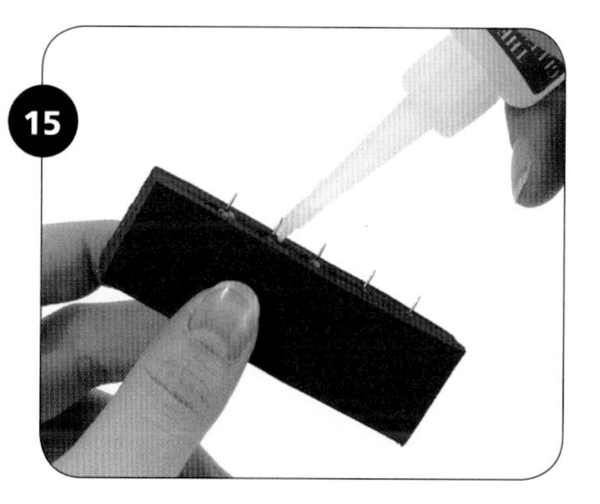

**15.** When the glue is dry, check to make sure that the pins do not move or shift position. If they do, drops of superglue applied at the head of each pin and where the pin exits the handle should hold them in place.

**16.** There should be 1/4-inch of each pin showing at the bottom of the handle. This is the "stripper" end of the handle. Cut a length of Foamies™ that is 3 inches x 1/2 inch.

**17.** Push the pin end of the handle into this strip to protect fingers from getting pricked by the pinpoints when you're not using your *lauhala* stripper

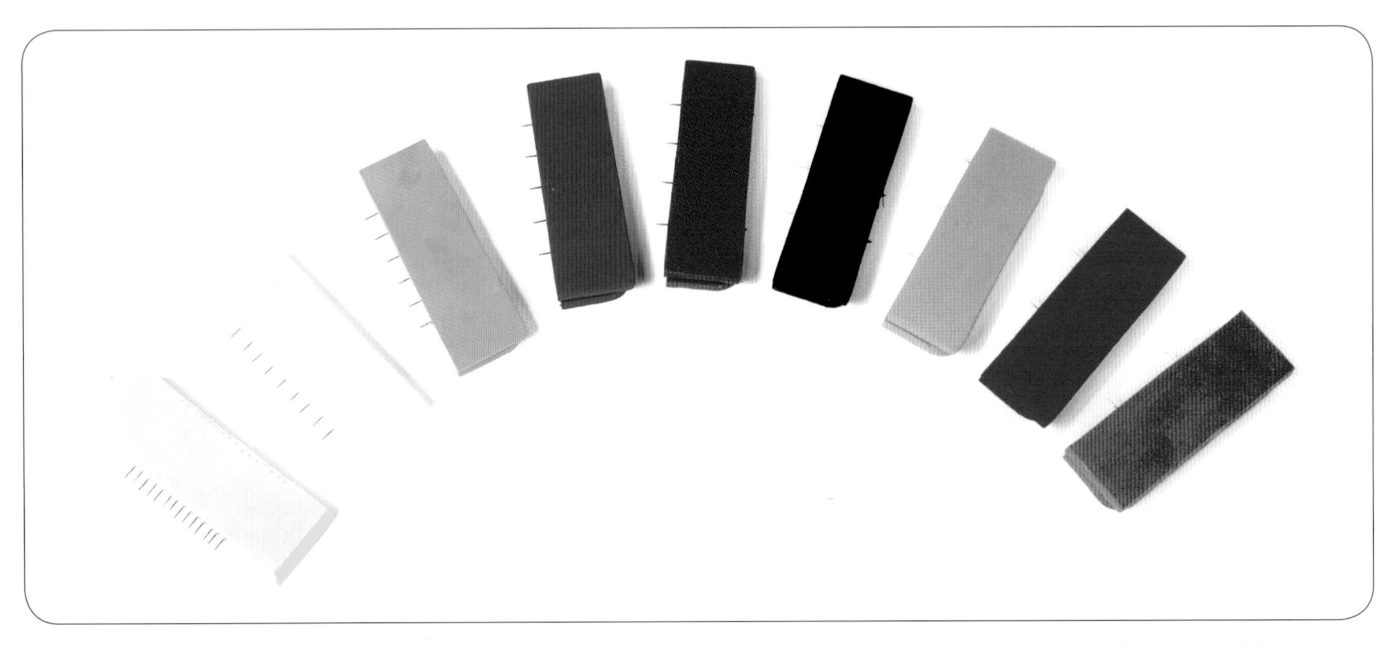

Here are nine strippers with varied spacing: Yellow - 1/8″ White - 1/4″ Green - 3/8″ Blue - 1/2″ Purple - 5/8″ Black - 3/4″ Orange - 7/8″ Red - 1″ Pink - 1-1/8″

You can make more strippers to cut different widths of *lauhala* strips. I recommend spacing the cuts every square (1/8-inch spacing), every three squares (3/8 inch), and every two squares (1/4 inch), in addition to the 1/2 inch spacing (every four squares) that you finished above.

You will also use your stripper to make the foundation (the band) of your bracelet. If your bracelet is 1-inch wide, then make a stripper handle with 2 pins, 8 squares apart (1 inch)—(see step #13). For 1-1/4 inch width, make a stripper handle with two pins, 10 squares apart (1-1/4 inch). For a 3/4-inch wide bracelet, make a stripper handle with two pins, 6 squares apart.

# Preparing Lauhala

## Ancient Knowledge from the Past

In the following projects you will learn how to select, gather, and clean hala leaves found in public areas and on hotel grounds. You will learn how to make or find the basic tools that any *lauhala* weaver needs and uses. The softening of the cleaned hala leaf is vital for a successful weaving experience. You will learn this valuable technique so that you can weave with soft, flexible *koana* (prepared *lauhala* strips cut to size).

## Selecting and Gathering *Lauhala*

Look at any hala tree and see if you can discover several curious things about the tree:

1. The leaves grow in a huge spiral around the trunk of the tree.
2. The long green leaves seem to stick up into the air, then, about a third of the way out, seem to fold down from the weight of the remaining length of the leaf.
3. There are rows of tiny thorns along the outer edges of the leaf and along the middle of the underside of the leaf.
4. Pineapple-shaped fruit seem to grow on these trees.
5. There are very thick, sturdy air roots growing from the trunk of the tree into the ground.

Stand under the tree and look up into the branches and instead of the beautiful green leaves you see old, dirty, dried-up brown leaves still attached to the trunk of the tree. These are the leaves you'll want to harvest for your *lauhala* projects. Wear sturdy gloves or use a thick towel to pull these brown leaves from the trunk. You can also look through the leaves that have recently fallen on the ground. Select the longest leaves that are fully intact. All of the leaves will have to be cleaned. Be careful not to get caught by the toothed spines on the leaf edges. Gather about a dozen leaves.

## Cleaning *Lauhala*

Cut off the thick *po'o lau* (leaf base) and use it as a tool to scrape out the mass of dirt accumulated in the deep fold of the leaf. Gather up your partially cleaned leaves and tie them together using another hala leaf. Take them back home.

The next time you plan to go to the ocean, take your hala leaves with you. Wash the hala leaves by swirling them individually in the ocean to remove the rest of the dirt, insects, and bird droppings.

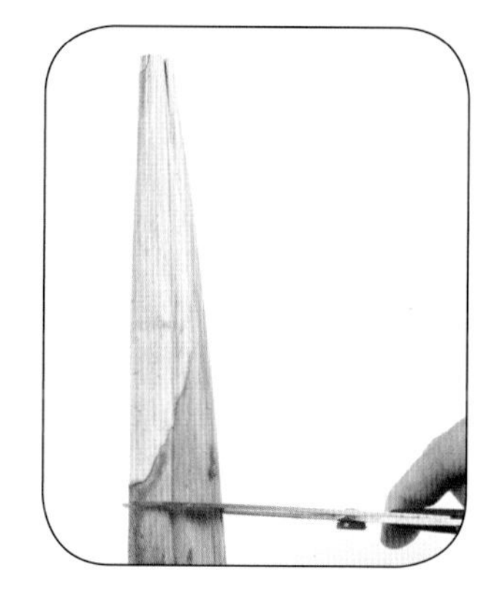

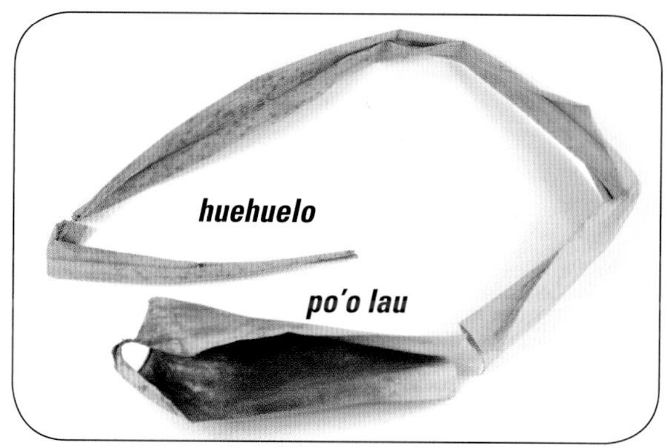

## Dethorning *Lauhala*

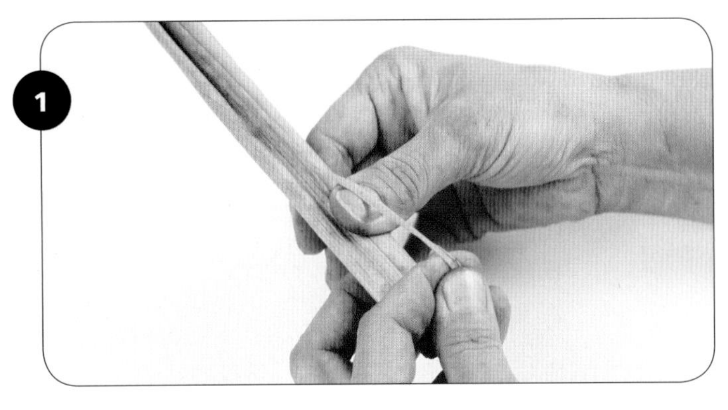

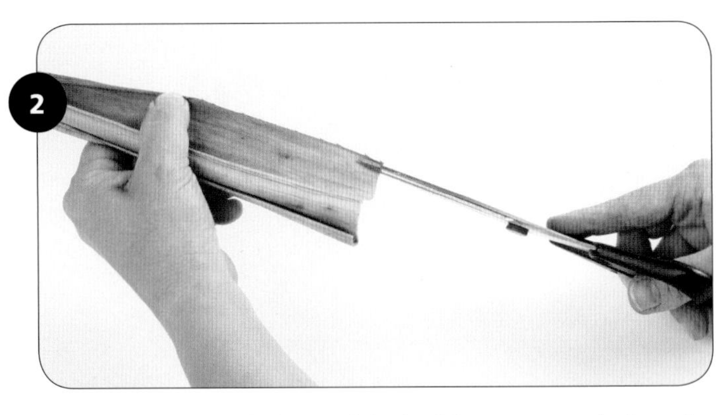

**1-2.** Remove the *huehuelo* (tip of the leaf) and any imperfections in the leaf. Beginning at the base of the leaf, insert your awl, pin-tool, sharp-pointed fish bone, or thumb nail into the butt of the leaf about a quarter of an inch inside the toothed leaf edge and carefully slit away the thorny strip from *po'o lau* (base) to *huehuelo* (tip). Remove the thorny strip from both edges of the leaf. You can also use a pair of scissors to carefully cut away the outer 1/4-inch strip from both leaf edges.

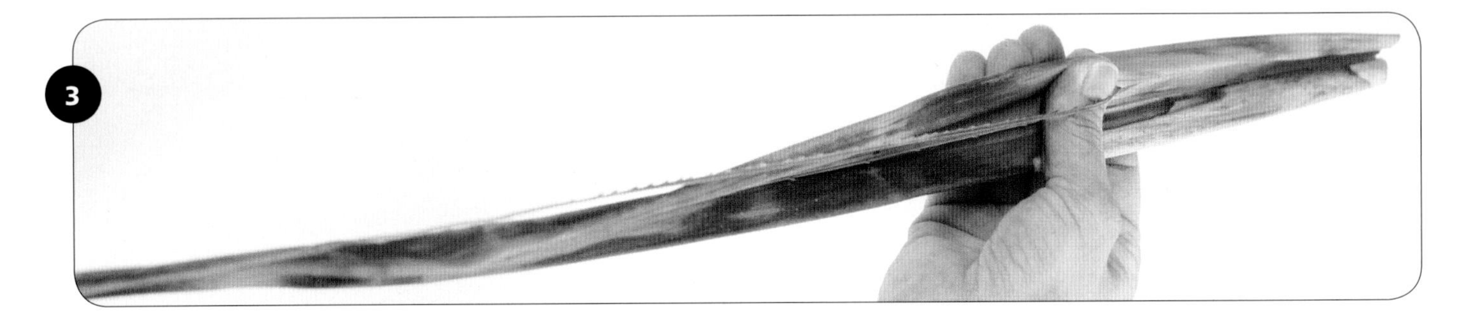

**3.** There is also a toothed edge on the underside of the leaf running down the midrib located in the middle of the leaf.

It is possible to separate this toothed edge from the midrib without actually cutting the midrib itself. This is a task, though, that will take lots of practice. For now, it is okay if you cut the midrib since our bracelets will be thinner than one-half of the full leaf width.

**4-5.** Next, using a traditional *'opihi* shell scraper or scissors, remove any thorns still left from the edges and midrib.

**6.** In earlier times, pieces of *tapa* (bark cloth) were used for the final cleaning of the leaf. Today, we can use a soft, moist face towel for this task.

Now we must soften and flatten the *lauhala* and roll them up into small storage rounds so that the leaves are protected until we are ready to cut them into our weaving strips.

## Softening *Lauhala*

In order to limber up *lauhala*, it must be worked and stretched to make the fibers elastic. Soak the leaves in hot water or seawater for 30 minutes to 1 hour. Always start at the butt end of the leaf with the thicker cuticle side up.

Which side is the thicker cuticle side?

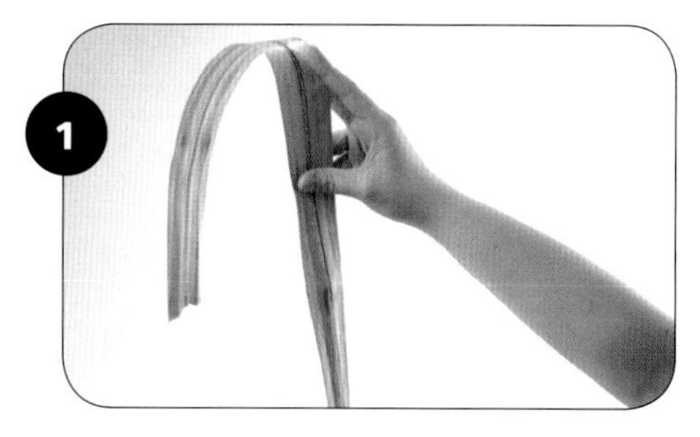


**1.** Hold the leaf by the butt end and observe which way *lauhala* curves naturally. The upper side of the natural curl of *lauhala* is the thicker cuticle side. The leaf will curl away from the thicker cuticle side.

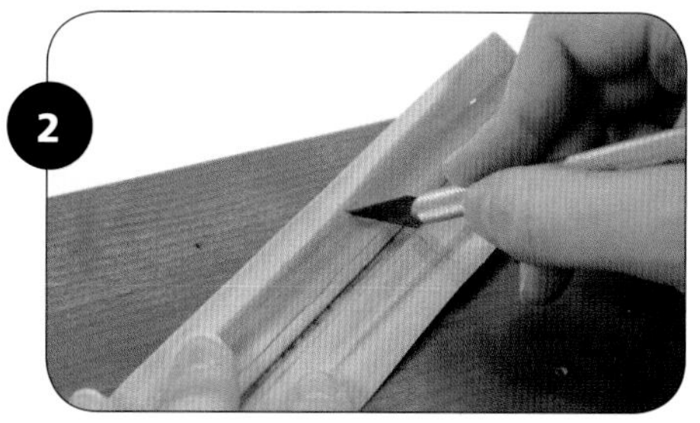


**2.** To test which side is the cuticle side, slice through half the thickness of the leaf.

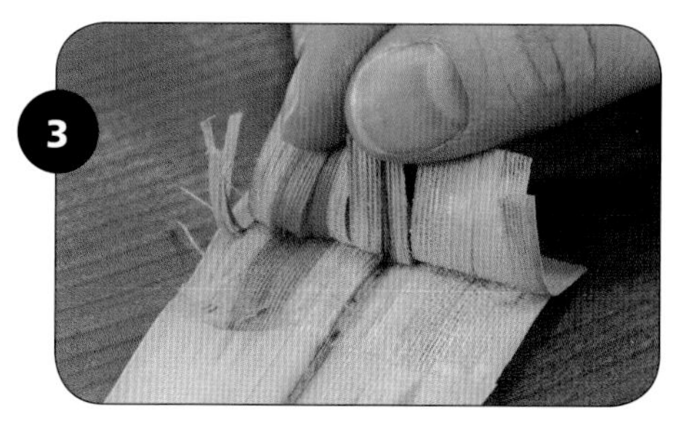


**3.** If you can peel back the meat of the leaf, then you did not cut through the stronger cuticle which is on the other side of the leaf. Flip the leaf over, choose a different spot on the leaf and test again to confirm from which side the meat easily separates.

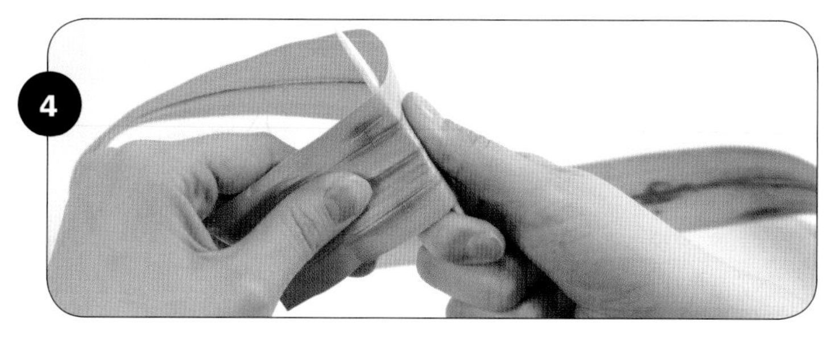


**4.** With the cuticle side up, pull the leaf, base first, over the back of the blade of a bread-and-butter knife or a bone awl (pictured). Start by just slightly bending the leaf around the knife or dowel.

**TIP:** *When you bend and stretch* lauhala *over the edge of a table or the back of a bread and butter knife, the thicker cuticle side must be up, otherwise the leaf will split.*

**TIP #2:** *You will bend and stretch each hala leaf 6 to 10 times over the knife back or table, each time increasing the angle to the knife back or table edge.* ***This is <u>the</u> most important step in preparing* lauhala *for weaving. If the* lauhala *is not limber, it will feel brittle and will crack and tear as you weave.***

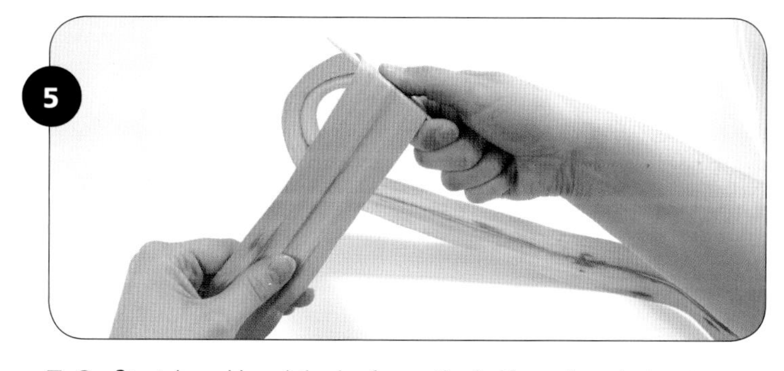


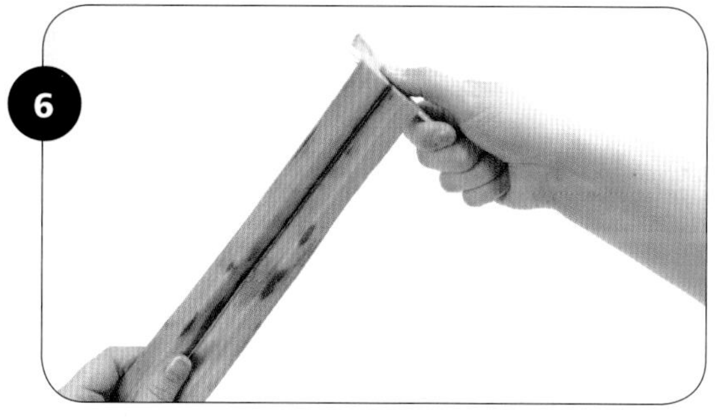


**5-6.** Stretch and bend the leaf over the knife or dowel at a steeper angle. You're pulling the leaf with one hand and adding resistance with the other hand by the pressure from your thumb on the leaf where it pulls across the back of the knife.

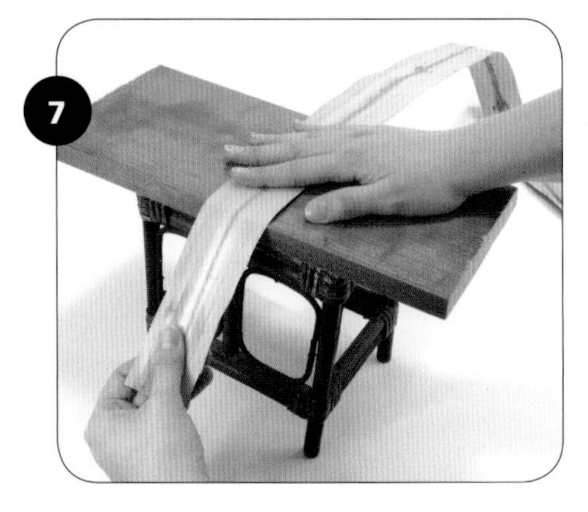


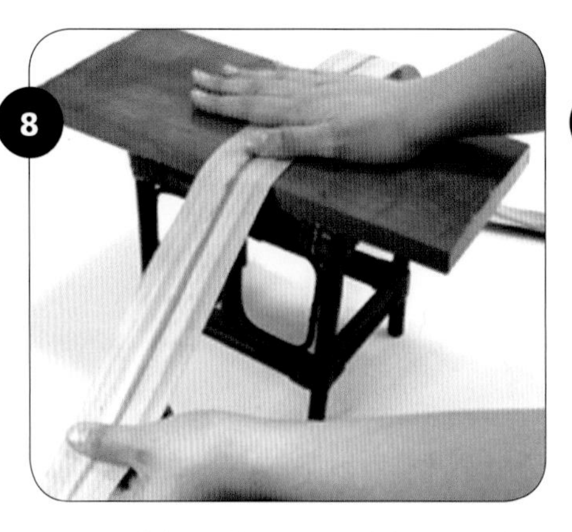

**7-8.** Some weavers like to pull the leaf over the edge of the table to stretch it and make it limber. Once again, one hand is pulling the leaf, from the base to the tip, while the other hand is applying resistance to the leaf where it bends around the edge of the table. Make sure the cuticle side is up, and gradually increase the bend each time you pull the leaf over the edge of the table.

**9.** Increase the angle of the leaf as you repeatedly draw it over the edge of the table. Make sure the cuticle side remains up.

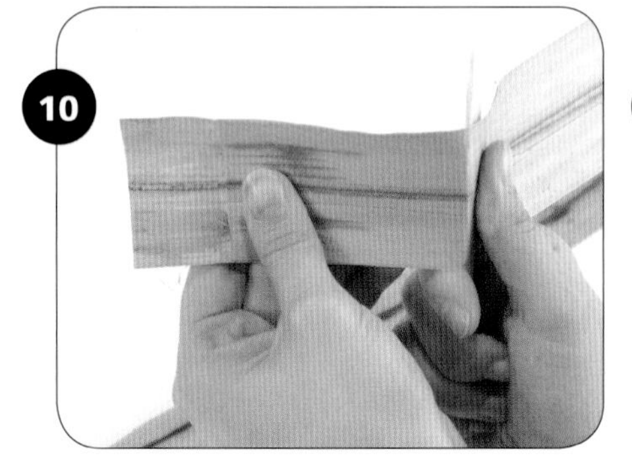

**10.** When the leaf feels pliable, flip it over and pull it over the knife, dowel or table edge with the cuticle side down. If the leaf starts to separate, stop and flip the leaf back over and work it some more with the cuticle side up.

**11.** Color the cuticle side of the butt end of the leaf with a red marker. This way, when we strip the leaf into *koana* we will still be able to tell which side needs to be "up."

When you have processed several leaves and they are dry, roll the softened and flattened leaves into a round for safe storage.

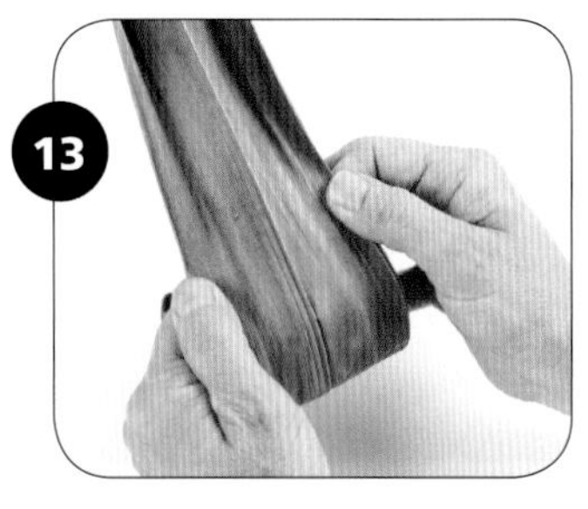


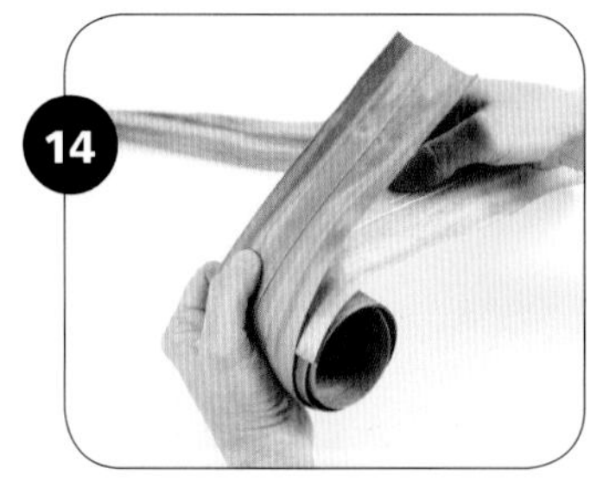

**12.** Roll the leaf, cuticle side in, around your fingers.

**13.** As you roll, pull the edges of the leaf out to flatten the leaf.

**14.** Insert the butt of a new leaf into the round so that there is a 6- to 8-inch overlap, with the cuticle side to the inside of the roll.

**15.** A round of about 20 leaves tied with a strip of *lauhala*.

## Stripping *Lauhala*

**1.** Place your prepared hala leaf on a piece of thick cardboard or dense packing Styrofoam, cuticle (red-marked) side up.

**2.** Measure two inches from the wider, thicker basal end of the leaf.

**3.** Push your 1/4-inch stripper into the leaf so that the stripper is at right angles to the length of the leaf.

**4.** Hold the wider, basal end of the leaf and pull slowly away from the pins. At the same time, push the stripper against the leaf.

**5.** Slowly pull the base of the leaf away from the stripper until the rest of the leaf is pulled through the pins.

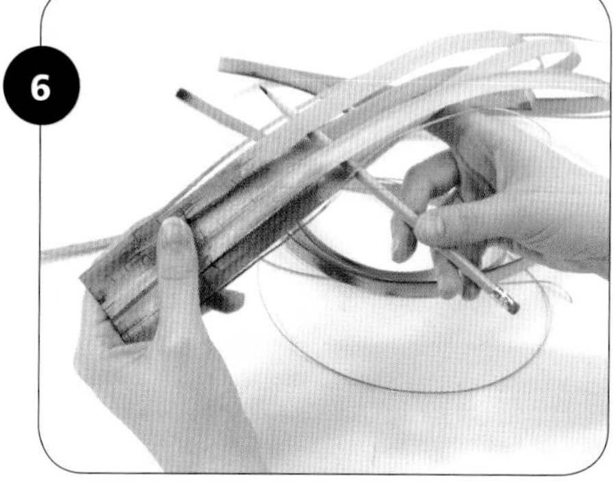


**6.** Align the pins so you strip the leaf along the leaf veins (the natural long lines within the leaf). Do not let the pins cross the veins. You want to have naturally straight strips of *lauhala*.

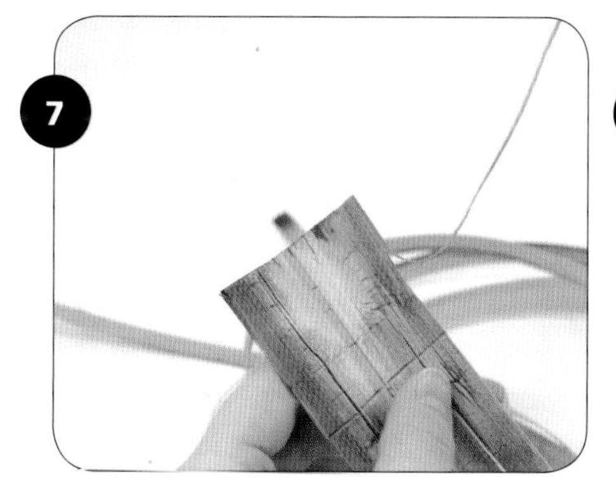


**7.** One pass through the stripper should give you 3 to 4 weaving strips. Strip several leaves until you have a number of beautiful, parallel-edged, uniform width strips. Align all of the butt ends of your newly crafted weavers.

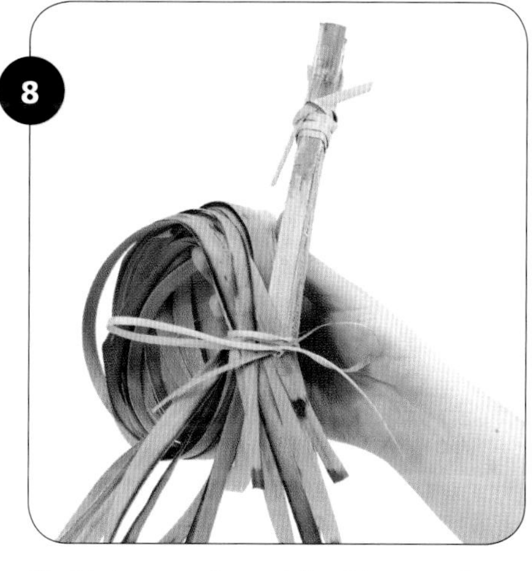


**8.** Make sure the cuticle sides are all visibly marked with the red band on the cuticle side. Tie them together at the butt end with a length of *lauhala*.

# Bracelet Foundation Coil

Locate the longest, most beautiful leaf in your round. We will make the bracelet foundation 1 inch wide. Use your pin stripper that has two pins one inch apart.

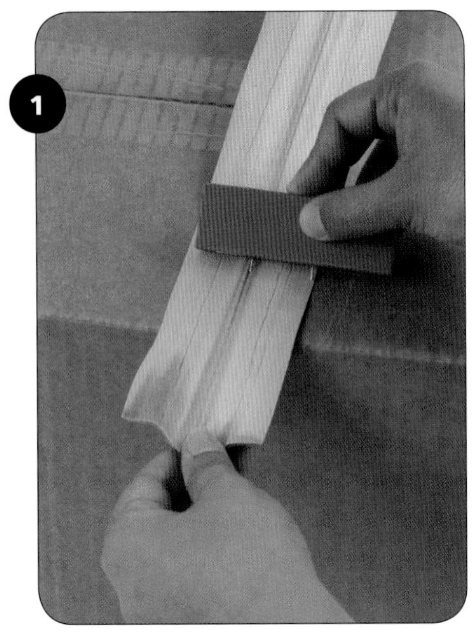


**1.** Lay the leaf on the thick cardboard or Styrofoam surface with the cuticle side up. Center the pin stripper over the base of the leaf, about 2 inches from the end.

**2.** Push the pins into the leaf so that the stripper is at right angles to the length of the leaf. Hold the wider, basal end of the leaf and pull slowly away from the pins.

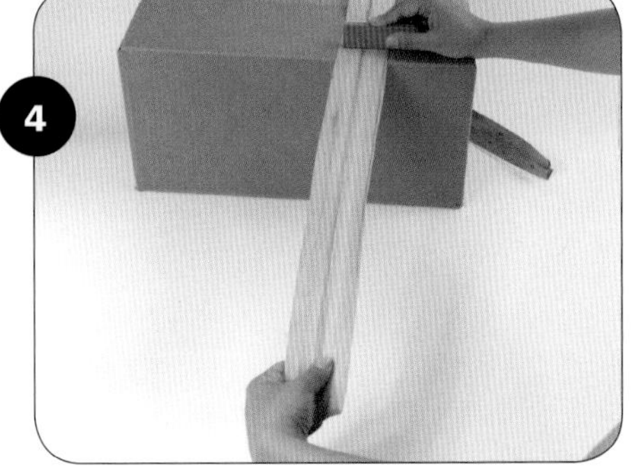


**3-4.** At the same time, push the stripper against the leaf as you slowly pull the base of the leaf away from the stripper until the rest of the leaf is pulled through the pins. Align your pins so you strip the leaf along the leaf veins (the natural long lines within the leaf).

**5.** Remove the two outer scrap pieces by cutting or carefully stripping them away with your fingers.

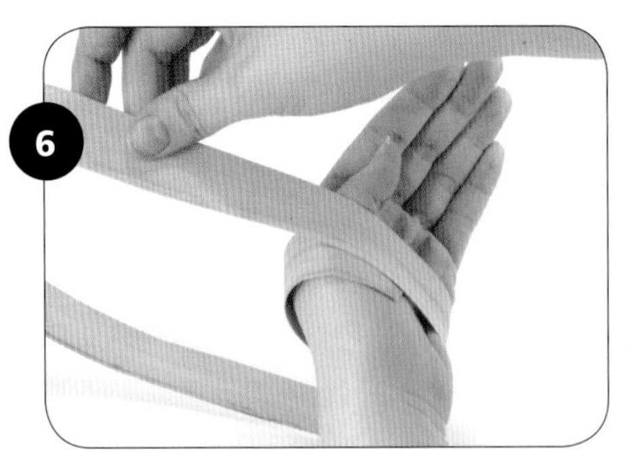


**6.** Make a fist with your thumb inside your fist and wrap the butt end (*cuticle side up*) of the leaf around the widest part of your fist (around the base of your thumb and little finger). Continue to wrap the leaf around itself until you have 14 inches of leaf left.

**7.** Carefully remove the bracelet coil from your fist and use a length of masking tape to hold the coil in place. Slip the coil back over your hand and onto your wrist to see if the coil is too tight or just right. Slip the coil off your wrist and check to make sure the individual plies of the coil are all uniform and against each other.

**8.** Lay the bracelet coil on the thick cardboard or Styrofoam surface with the cuticle side up

**9.** Pick up your 1/2-inch pin stripper that has three pins 1/2 inch apart and line it up so that you can split the leaf into two equal widths of 1/2 inch each. Center the pin stripper over the 14-inch leaf tail as close to the coil as possible without creasing the leaf.

**10.** Push the pins into the leaf so that you will create two warp strands (weaving elements) and two thinner outer strips.

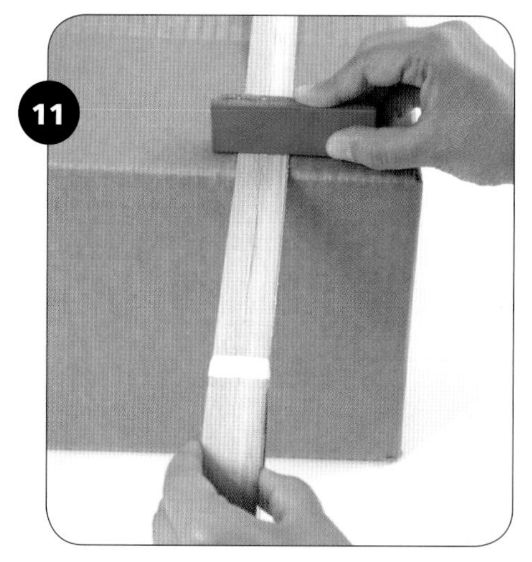


**11.** Hold the leaf at the base and slowly pull away from the pins. At the same time, push the stripper against the leaf as you pull the leaf away from the stripper so that the remainder of the leaf is pulled through the pins.

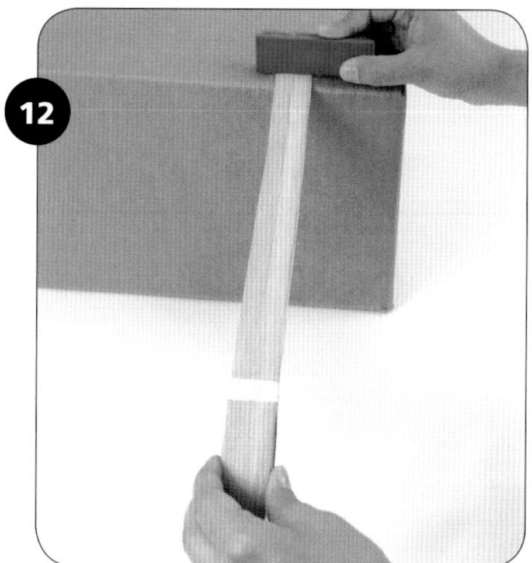


**12.** The coil should now have 2 uniform warp elements and two thinner strips on either side of the 2 warp elements.

**13.** Cut the two thinner elements off leaving the 2 warp elements. Dampen the coil and the 2 attached warp elements with the damp rag.

**TIP:** *While weaving, the cuticle side (the side that will be seen) should always be out, facing the viewer.*

**TIP:** *The following projects have been put in order of progressive difficulty. I recommend that you do the projects in order so that those steps you learn will help with each succeeding project. It is much easier to work with larger elements when learning to weave with lauhala. The first project has only two warp elements so that you learn to weave over and under while at the same time folding the warp elements back and forth to get the tightness in the weave. You will fold back against the weaving element you just completed so that there will be no space between the weaving rows. Each project will teach you an important lesson. When you finish the last project you will be an expert weaver, able to figure out any pattern and work with very thin weaving elements.*

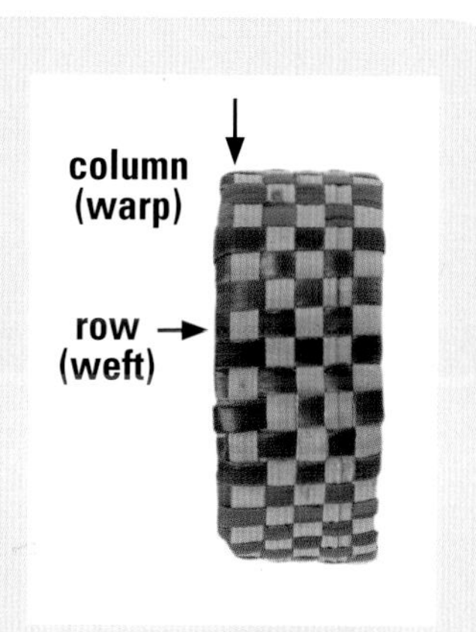

# Projects

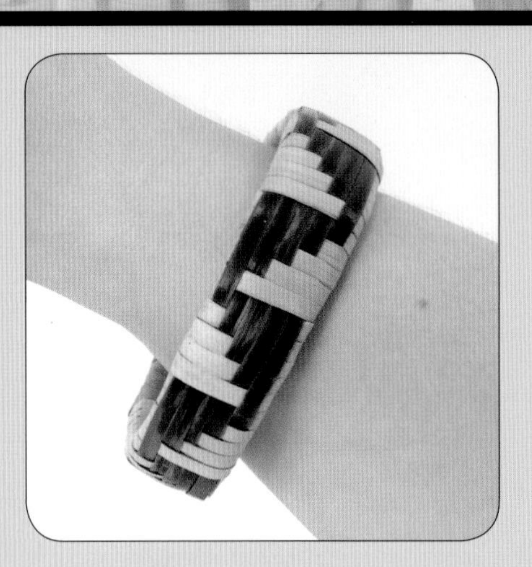

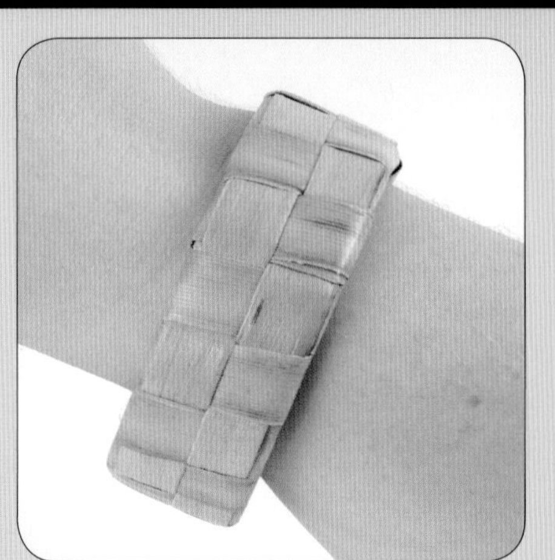

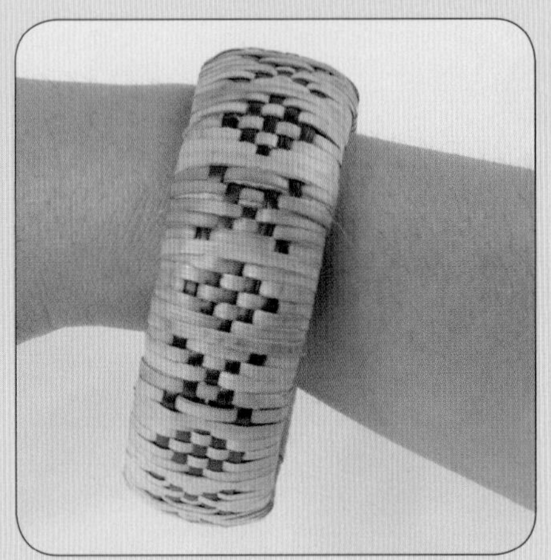

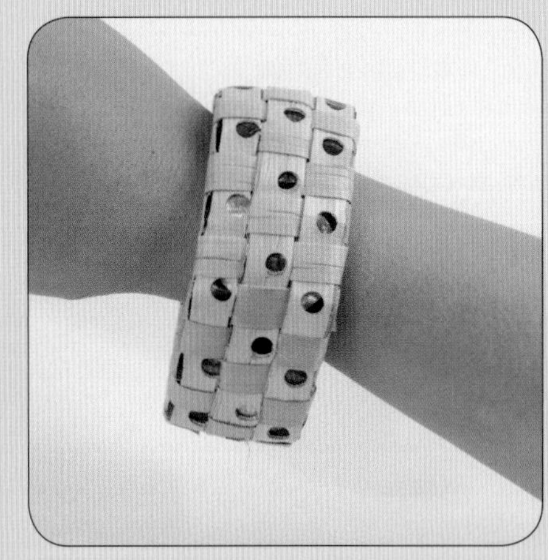

# *Project 1:* Checkerboard with 2 Warp Strands

**WHAT YOU'LL NEED:**
- cleaned and prepared *lauhala* strips
- scissors
- lauhala strippers
- masking tape
- awl or similar tool for lifting loops and making space to slide an element
- spray bottle with water to keep lauhala moist

**TIP**: *Keep your spray bottle handy and moisten the koana as needed. If the weaving elements feel dry, a quick pump of the spray bottle is necessary.*

## Weaving *Lauhala*

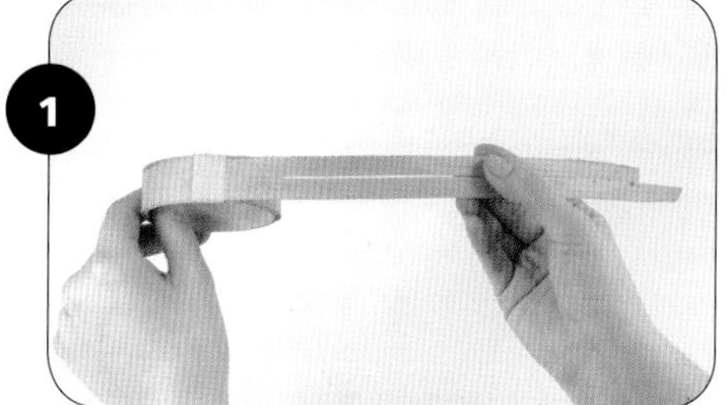

**1.** Hold your bracelet coil so that the 2 warp elements are horizontal and to the right of the coil.

**2.** Use your awl to make a space between the individual plies of the coil adjacent to the masking tape and the loose warp strands.

**TIP**: *The butt end of the koana is thick. As the leaf tapers to the end it becomes thinner and thinner. Don't wait until the leaf is too thin before splicing a new weaver into the bracelet. The thicker leaf is stronger and also looks better in the weaving.*

**3.** With the cuticle facing the center, slide the thicker end of the weft into the space between the plies of the coil until it emerges from the bottom of the coil.

**4.** Adjust the end of the weft so that it is vertical and sticks out from the bottom of the coil 3/4 inch.

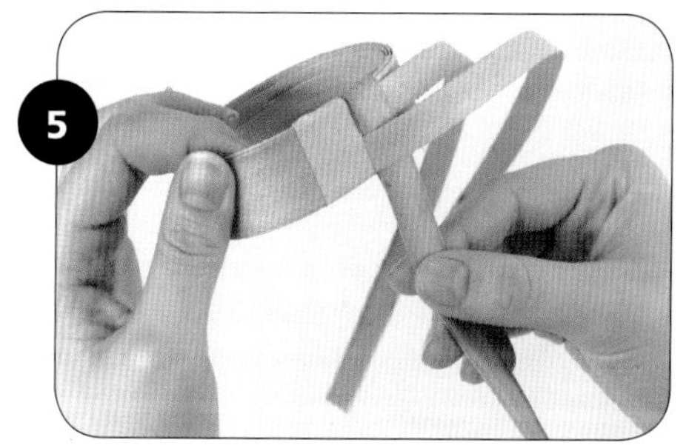

**5.** Row 1: Weave the long end of the weaving strand over the first warp strand (make sure that the cuticle side is now facing you) and then under the second warp strand.

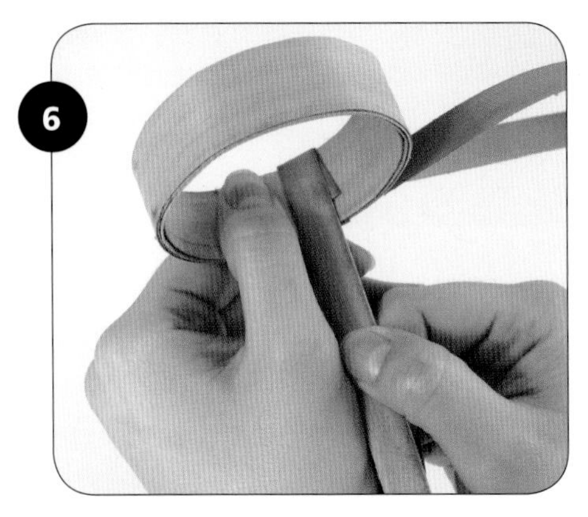


**6.** Wrap the weft to the inside of the coil, making sure to keep the short tailpiece aligned and hidden under the weft. Bring the weft through the inside of the coil to prepare for the next row of weaving.

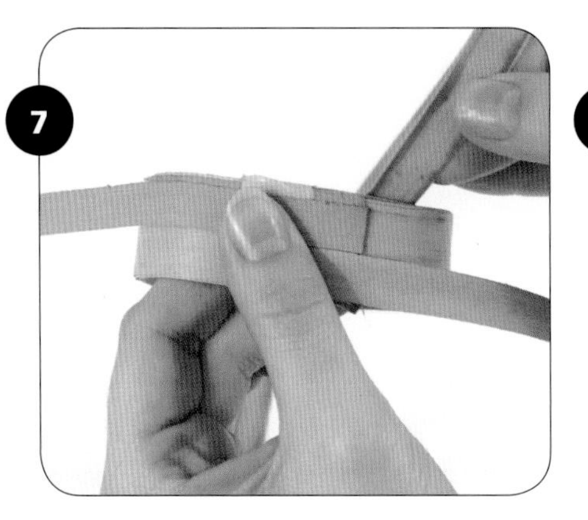


**7.** Row 2: Fold the first warp element back on itself and against the weft, which is covering it on the left.

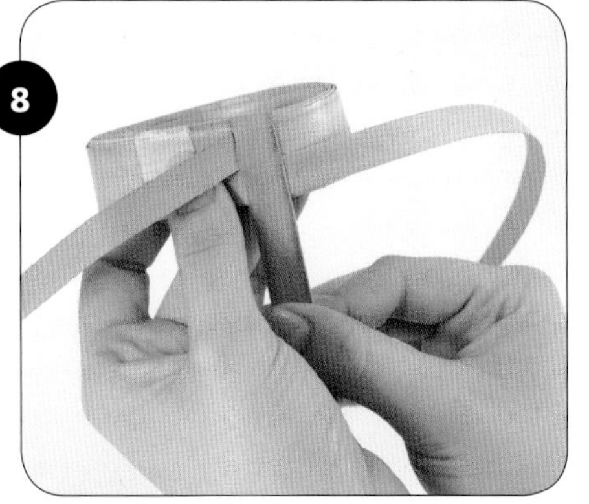


**8.** Bring the weft over the top of the coil and weave over the second warp element.

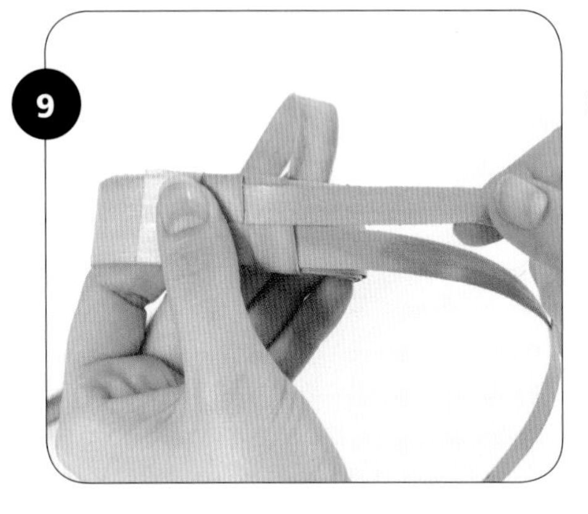


**9.** Unfold the first warp element and lay it over the weft. This completes Row 2.

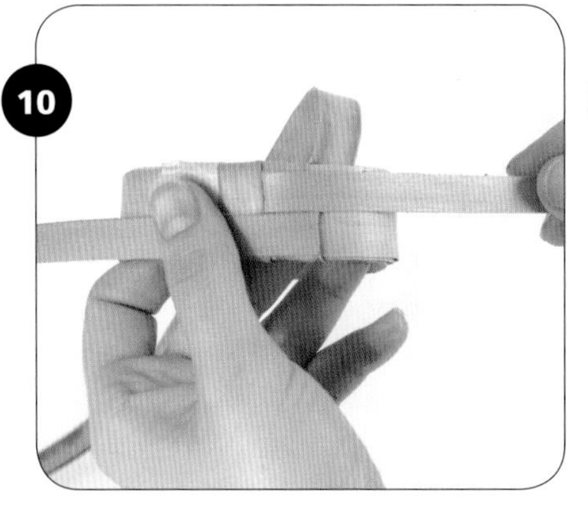


**10.** Row 3: Fold the second warp element back on itself and against the weft, which is covering it on the left.

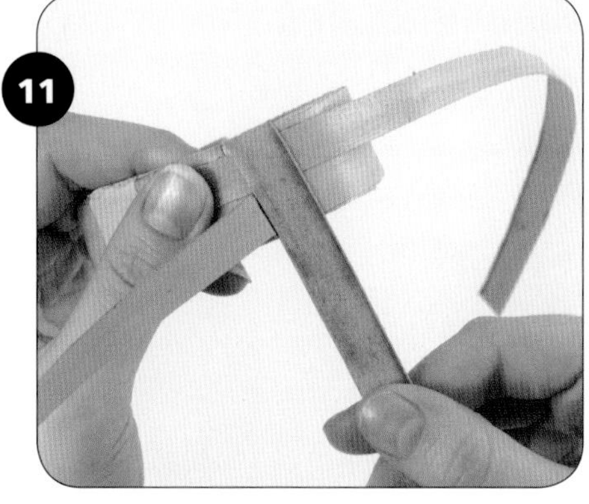


**11.** Bring the weft over the top of the coil and weave over the first warp element.

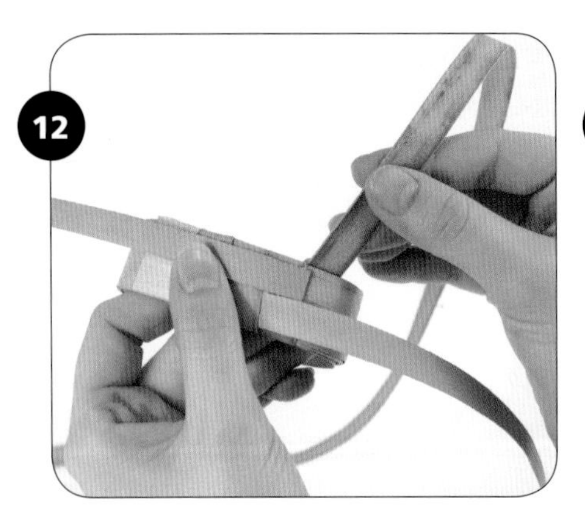


**12.** Row 4: Unfold the second warp element and lay it over the weft. This completes Row 3.

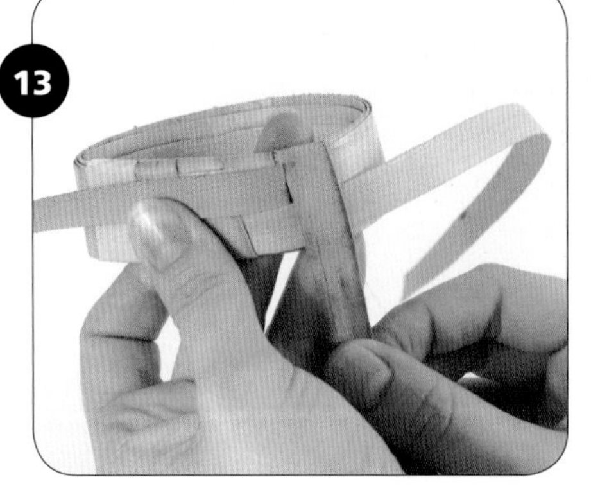


**13.** Row 4: Fold the first warp element back on itself and against the weft, which is covering it on the left.

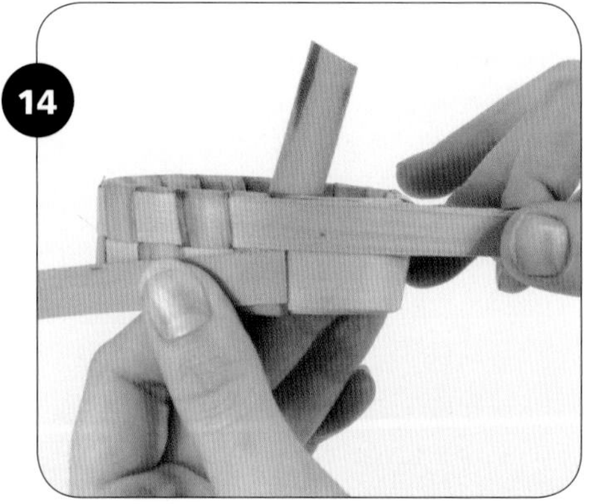


**14.** Bring the weft over the top of the coil. Our leaf has run out and we need to splice in a new weft so we can continue.

## Inserting a New Weft

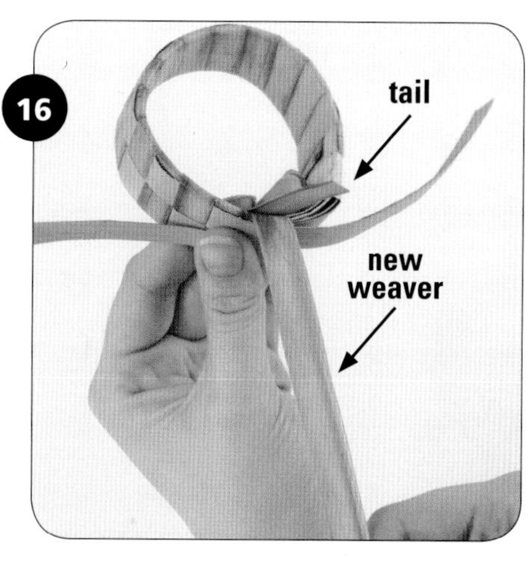


**15-16.** Slide the thicker end of the new weaving element, with the cuticle side up, into the space between the plies of the foundation coil.

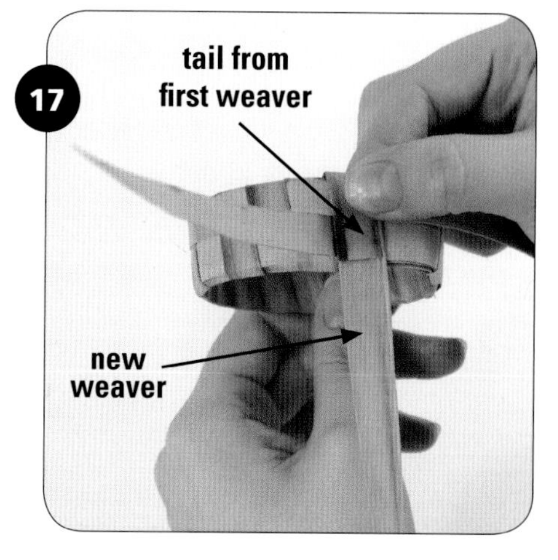


**17.** Fold both the new weft and the tail of the first weft over the first warp element. The second warp element will fold back over the new weft and the tail of the first weft. This completes Row 4.

Continue the pattern for the duration of the bracelet.

## Interweaving and Finishing

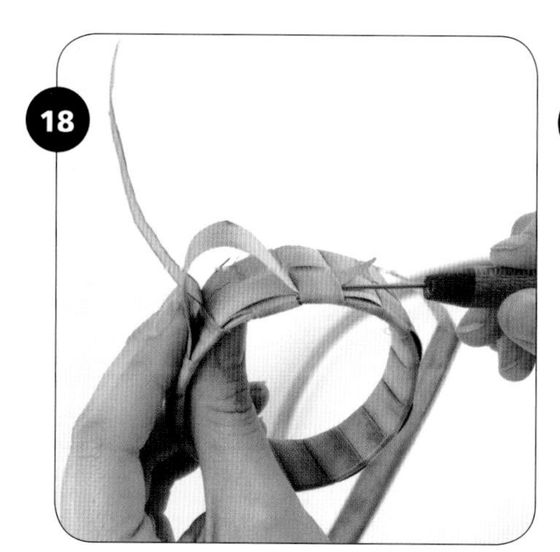

**18.** We are one weave short of the beginning. Use the awl to make a space under the first weft and slide the second warp strand into the weave and pull tight.

**19.** Fold the first warp strand back on itself and bring the weft down over the second warp strand.

**20.** Use the awl to make a space under the second weaving strand and slide the first warp strand into the weave and pull tight.

**21.** Now use the awl to make a space under the second warp strand and slide the weaving strand into the weave and pull tight.

**22.** The two warp strands and the weaving strand are all interwoven into the beginning of the bracelet and pulled tight.

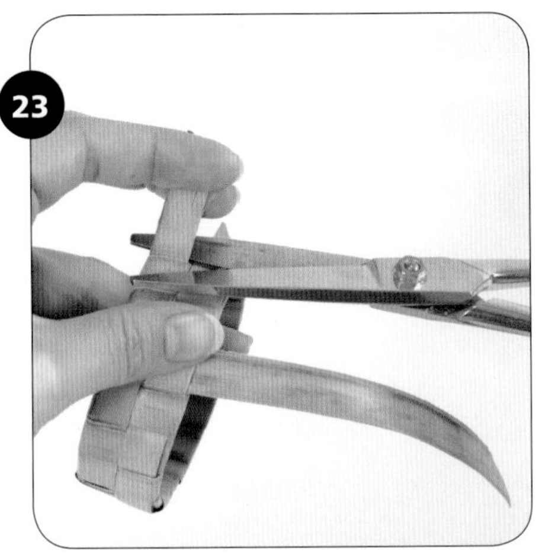

**23.** Trim the ends of the two warp strands by pulling taut and cutting, so that, when released, the end will disappear back into the weave.

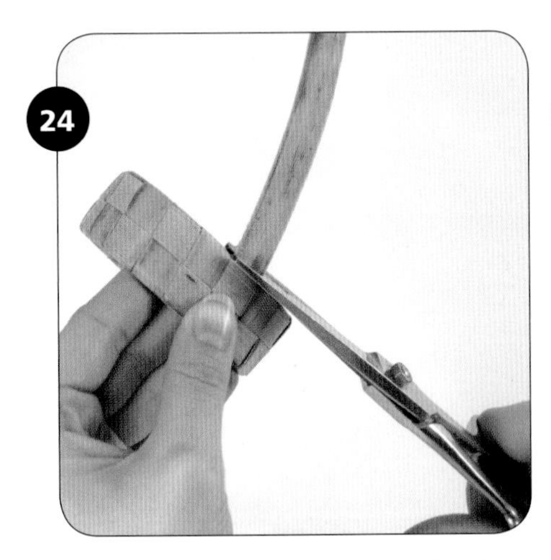

**24.** Trim the end of the weft with a sharp pair of scissors.

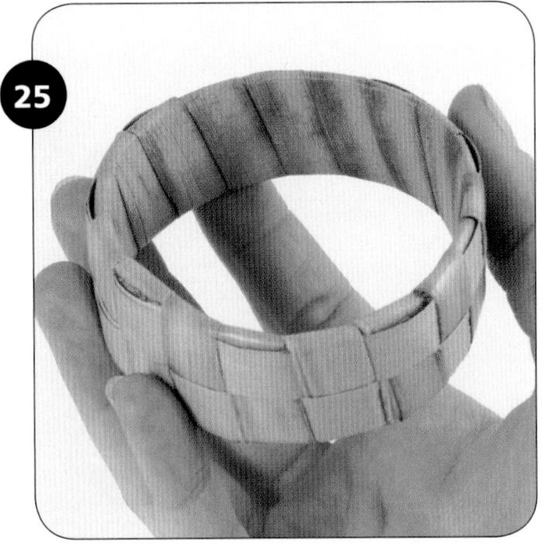

**25.** Check on the inside of the coil that your wraps are straight and next to each other. A well-woven bracelet will not show any of the original coil on the inside – only the wraps.

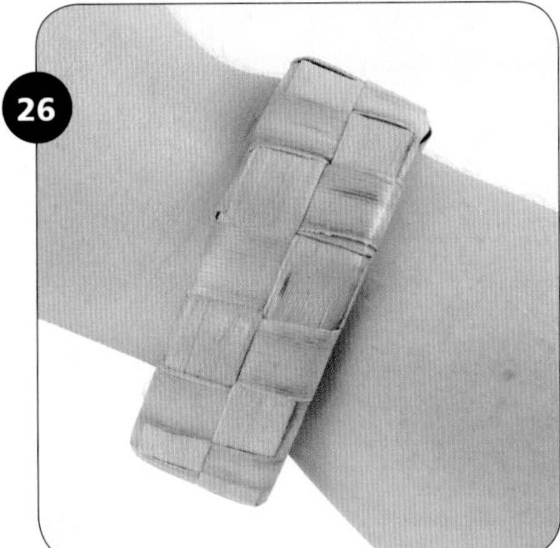

**26.** The completed bracelet project.

*Project 2:*

# Simple Embellishment #1

## Added to Project 1

**PREPARATION:**
You'll use the bracelet from Project 1.

**WHAT YOU'LL NEED:**
- 3/8-inch *koana*, or weaving strip. Use the 3/8-inch stripper

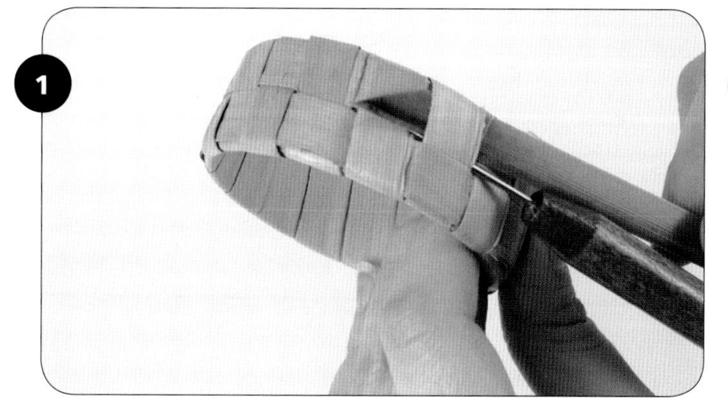

**1.** Using the bracelet from project one, insert the 3/8-inch *koana,* cuticle side down, under one weft. Use the awl to make a space for the strand. Pointing the end of the strand will help with the insertion.

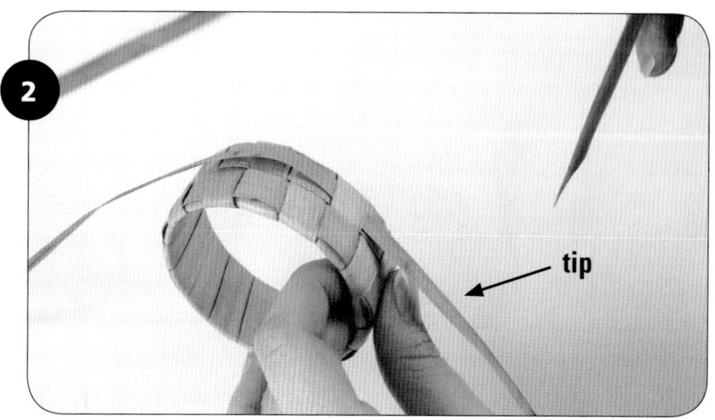


**2.** Pull the strand through the loop leaving a tail (tip) of the thinner, weaker part of the *koana.*

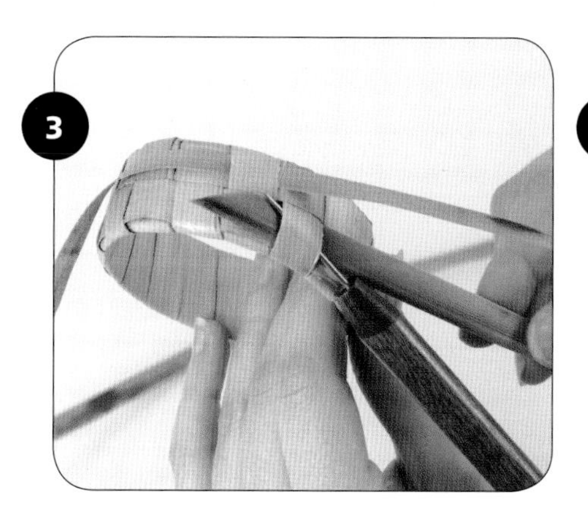

**3.** Fold the strand back on itself so the cuticle side is down and then insert it through the next loop, to the right and below the first loop. Always insert from the right to the left.

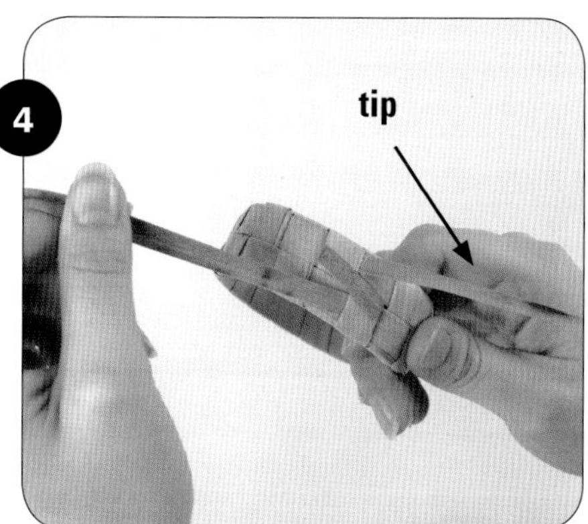


**4.** Pull the strand all the way through until the cross from the previous loop is tight.

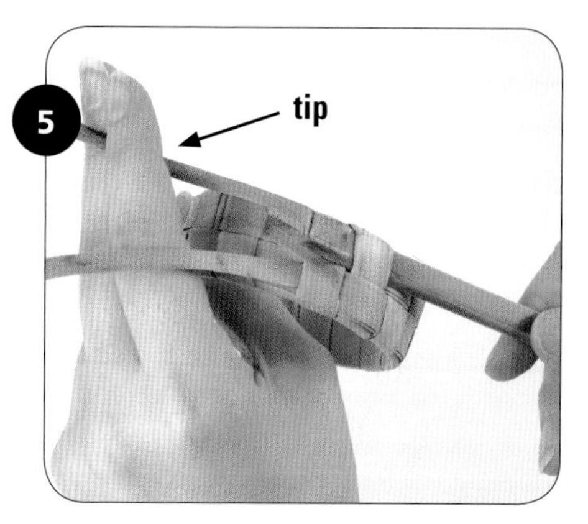


**5.** Fold the strand back on itself and inset it through the next loop to the right and above the second loop. Insert from the right to the left. Pull the strand all the way through until the cross from the previous loop is tight.

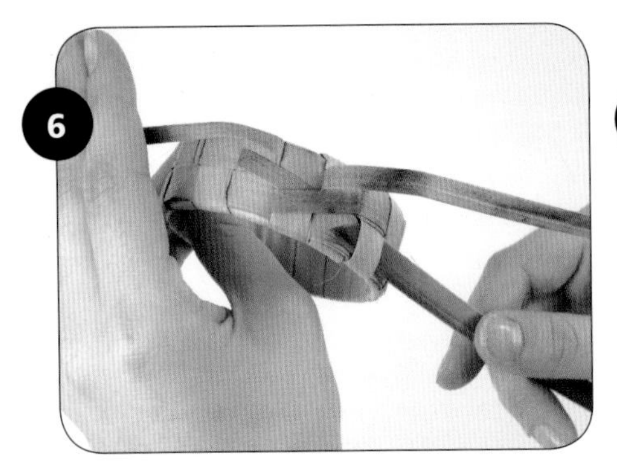


**6.** Fold the strand back on itself, then insert it through the next loop to the right and below the third loop. Insert from the right to the left. Pull the strand all the way through until the cross from the previous loop is tight.

**7.** Fold the strand back on itself, then insert it through the next loop to the right and above the fourth loop. Insert from the right to the left. Continue the pattern all the way around the bracelet.

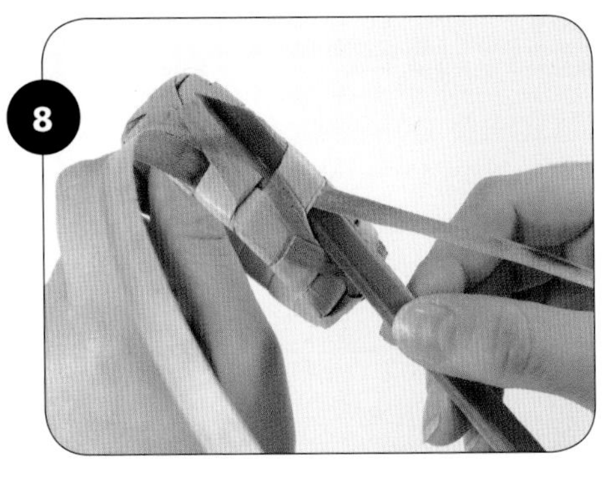


**8.** When you get back to the beginning, insert the strand under the beginning of this *koana*.

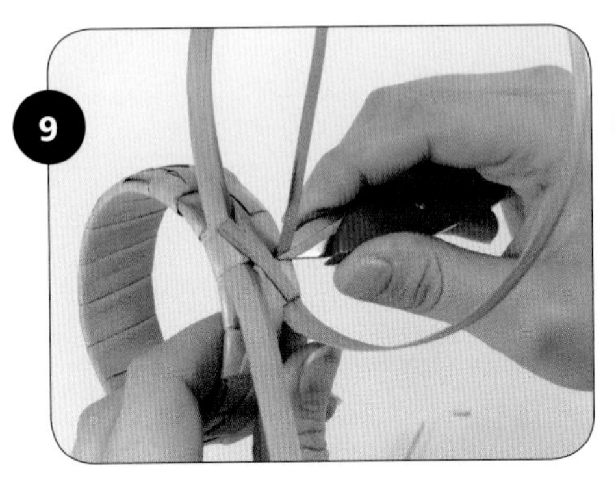


**9.** Trim the end of the beginning *koana*.

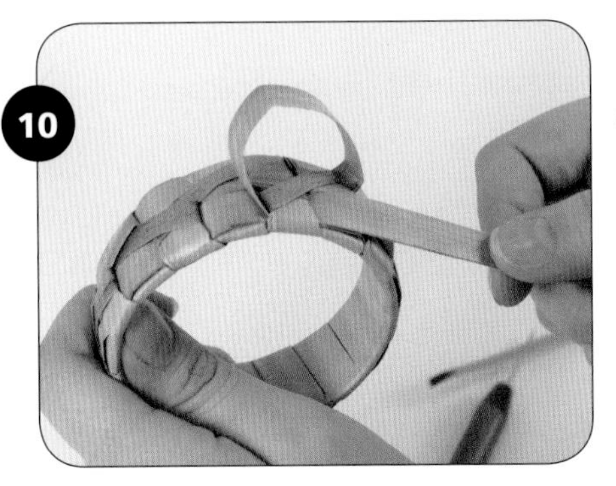


**10.** Continue weaving over the beginning *koana* for a few stitches to secure the weaving.

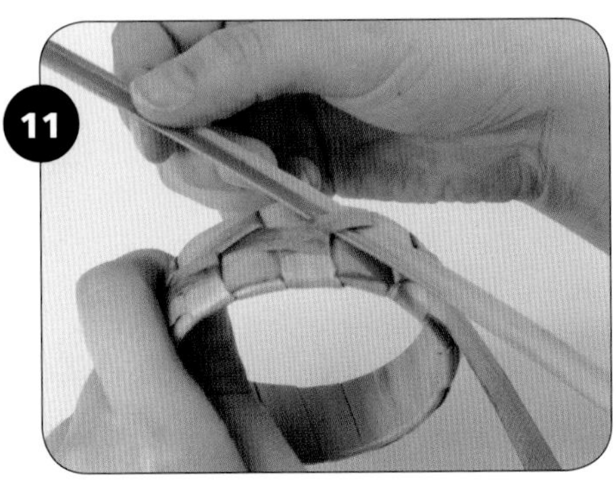


**11.** You may end the weaving either under the vertical stitch or the diagonal stitch.

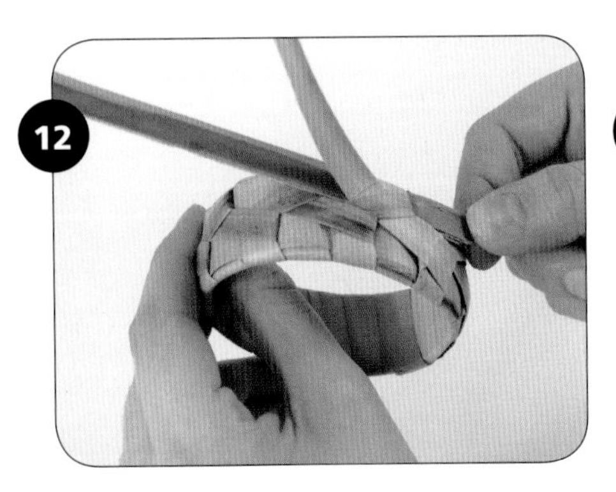


**12.** Since we've been weaving with the thicker butt end of the *koana*, we're using this thicker part of the leaf to cover the thinner leaf that wove the beginning stitches for a nicer look.

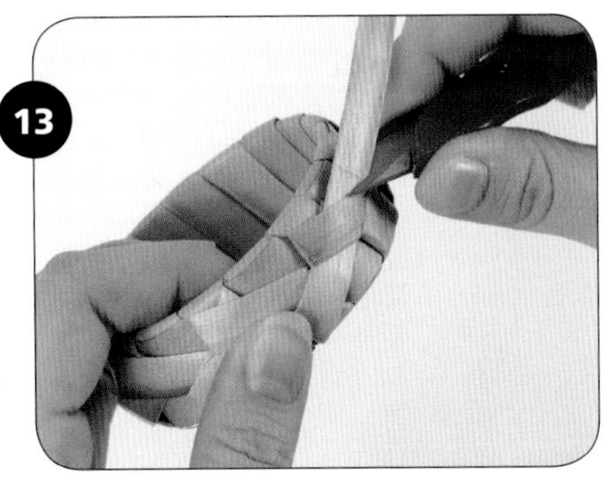


**13.** Pull the weaver taut, give it a slight stretch and trim the leaf. The end will pull back and disappear under the stitch.

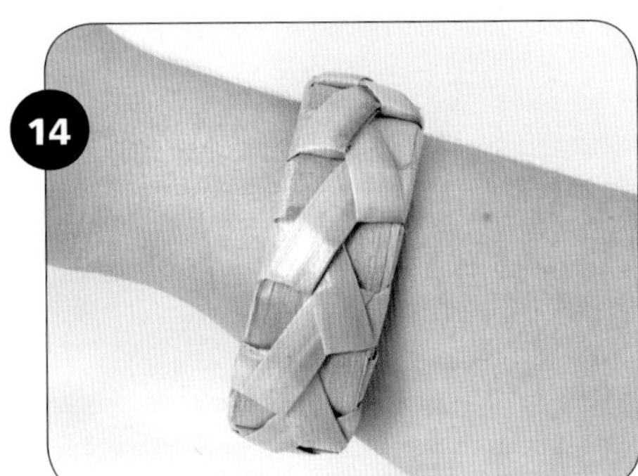


**14.** The completed bracelet project.

# *Project 3:* Three-Warp Checkerboard

## 3/8-inch Wide Warp and Weft

**PREPARATION:**
Make a foundation coil that is 1-1/8-inch wide. Strip the last 14 inches into three warp strands, 3/8-inch wide each. Strip another leaf into 3/8-inch wide weft strands.

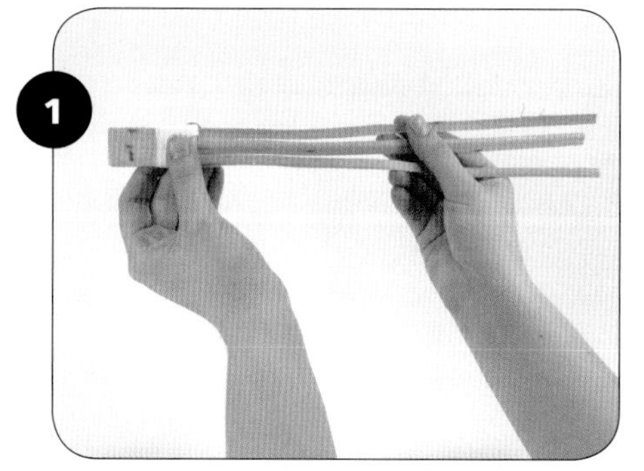

**1.** Hold your bracelet coil so that the 3 warp elements are horizontal and are to the right of the coil.

**2.** Use your awl to make a space between the individual plies of the coil adjacent to the masking tape and the loose warp strands.

**3.** With the cuticle facing the center, slide the thicker end of the weaver into the space between the plies of the coil until it emerges from the bottom of the coil. Adjust the end of the element so that it is vertical and sticks out 3/4-inch from the bottom of the coil.

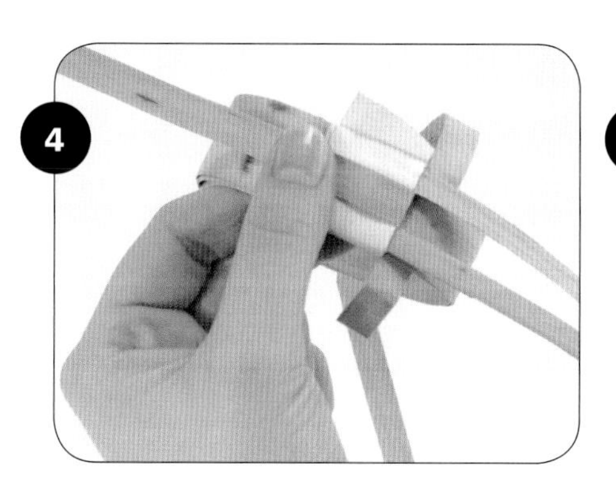

**4.** Row 1: Fold the middle warp strand back on itself.

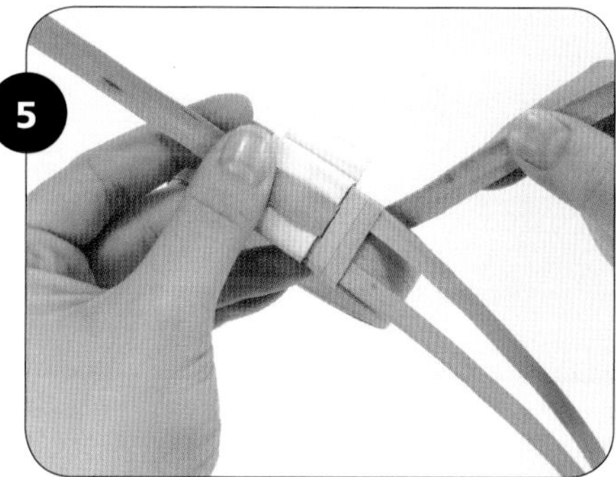

**5.** Weave the long end of the weaving strand over the first warp strand (make sure that the cuticle side is now facing you) and then across the space occupied by the second warp strand, then over the third warp strand.

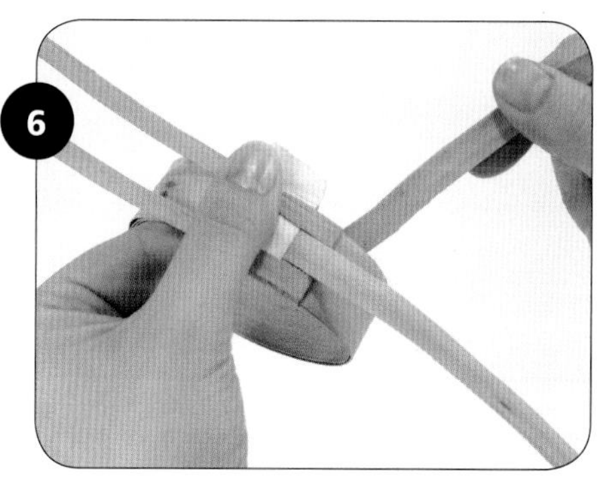

**6.** Wrap the weaver to the inside of the coil, making sure to keep the short tailpiece aligned and hidden under the weaver. Fold the middle warp strand back over the weaving strand. Fold the first and third warp strands back on themselves.

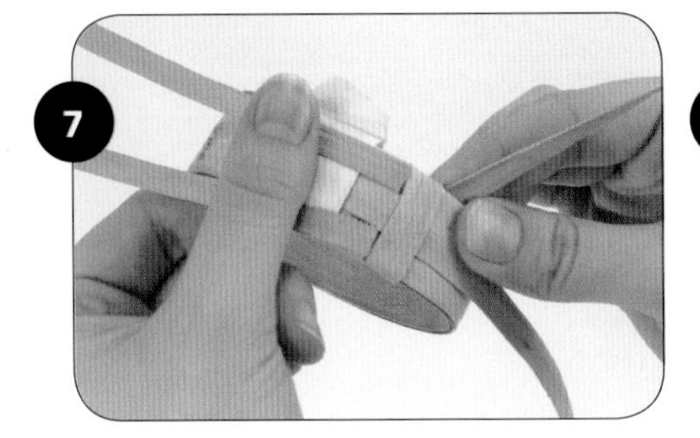

**7.** Row 2: Lay the weft strand over the space occupied by the first and third warp strands and over the middle warp strand.

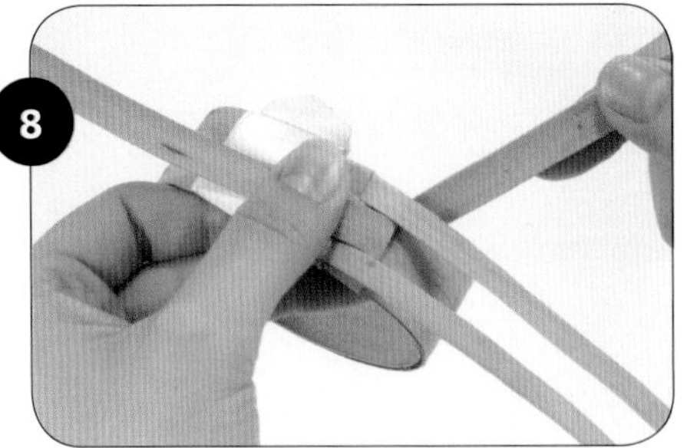

**8.** Fold the first warp strand and the third warp strand over the weaving strand and fold the middle warp strand back on itself.

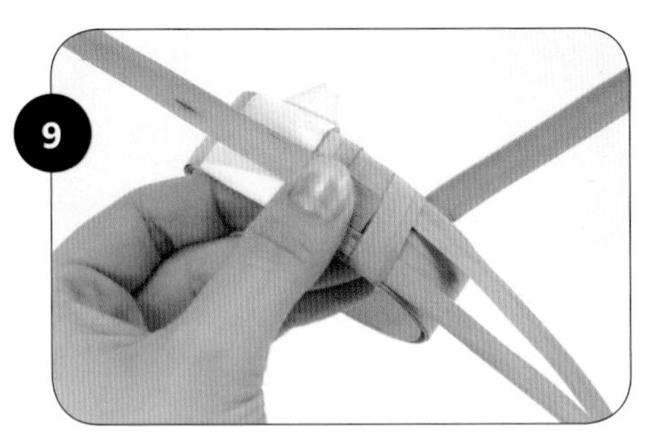

**9.** Row 3: Lay the weft strand over the first and third warp strand and over the space occupied by the middle warp strand.

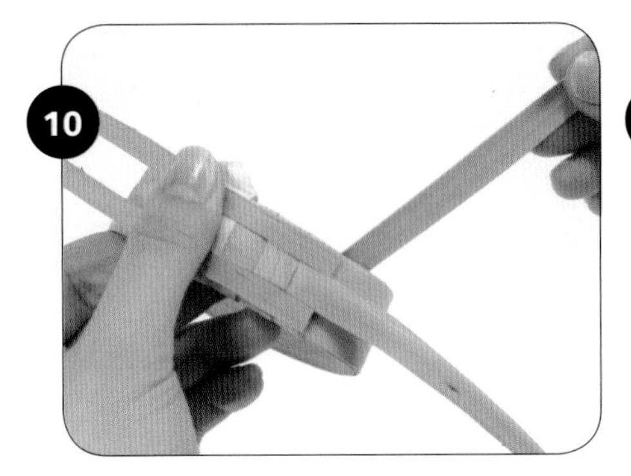

**10.** Continue weaving the pattern.

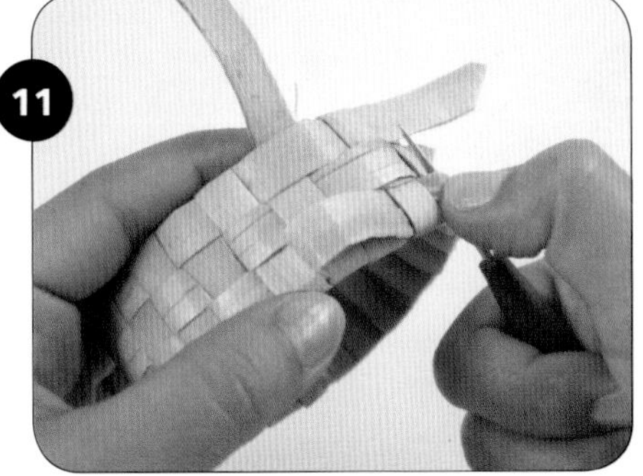

**11.** When you get to the end of the weaving you will interweave the ends of the warp strands into the beginning of the weave. Make sure you moisten both the warp and weaving strands so that you can stretch the loops to slide in the tips of the strands.

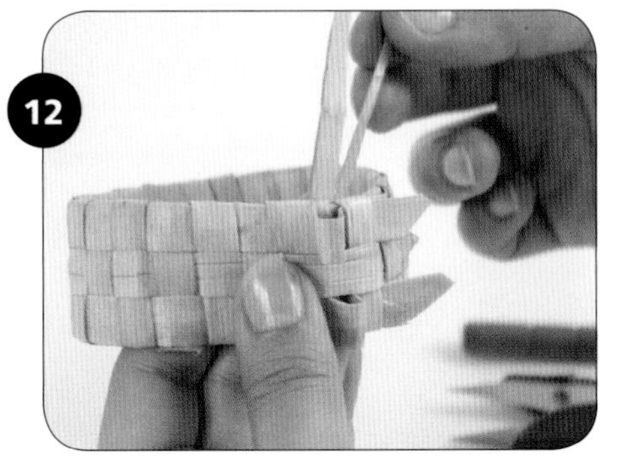

**12.** In this bracelet, the under-over pattern didn't quite fit in the remaining space so we cut the weaving strand in half, from the tip to where it bent over the edge of the foundation.

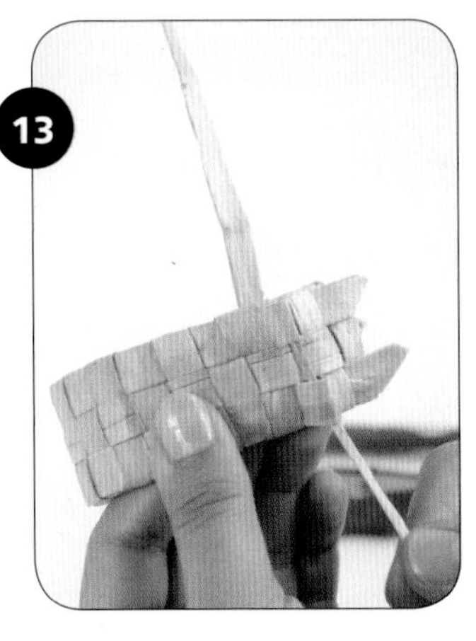

**13.** We wove the thinner weaving strip over the first (top) warp, under the second warp and over the third (bottom) warp strand.

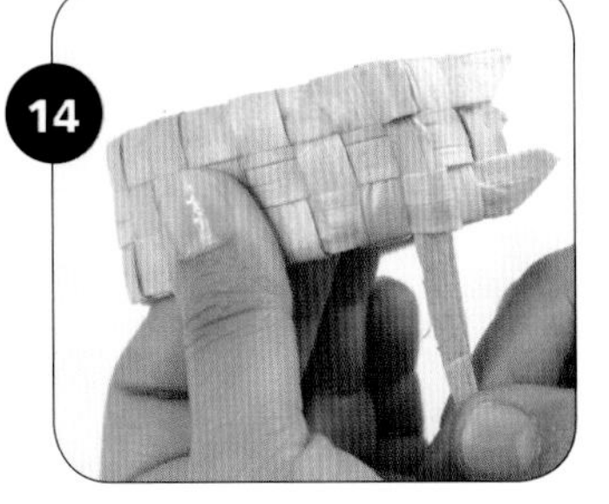

**14.** Then we wove the wider part of the weaving strip in the same space but on top of the thinner weaving strand. We continued by wrapping the wider weaving strand around the bracelet and interwove it into the next row so that it would be under the top (first) warp, over the middle warp and under the bottom (third) warp strand to secure it.

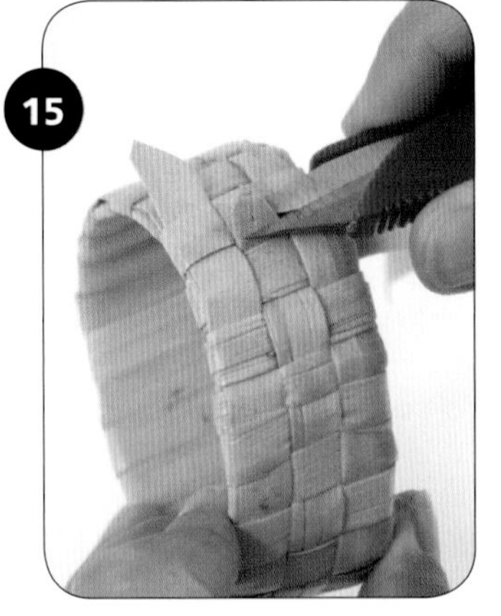

**15.** Pull the three warp strands snug and trim the ends.

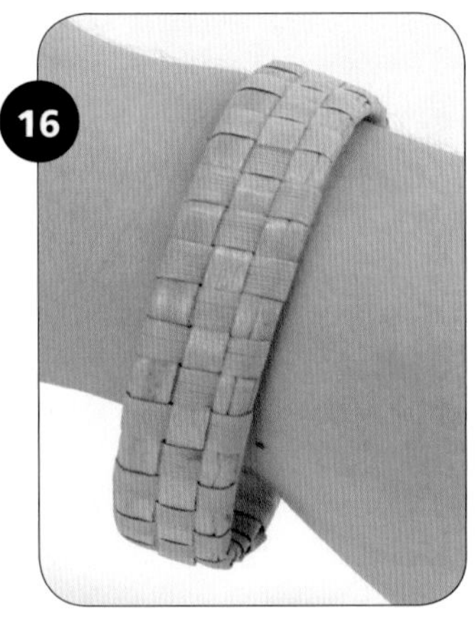

**16.** The completed bracelet project.

# Project 4:
# Simple Embellishment #2
## Added to Project 3

**1.** Using the bracelet from Project 3, insert a new *koana,* 3/8-inch wide, cuticle side down under the middle warp strand and pull it through until you have a tail of 2 inches.

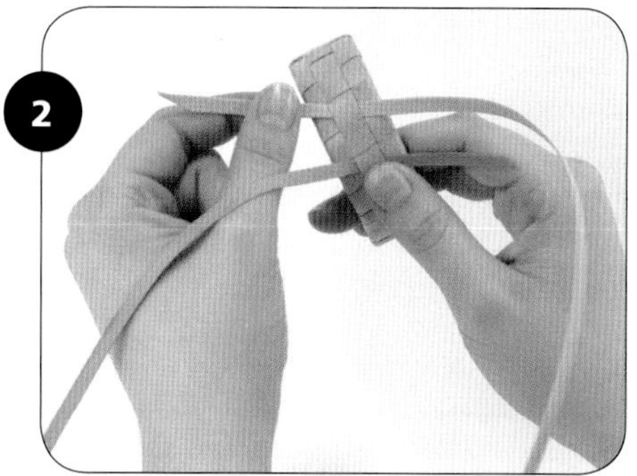


**2.** Insert the end of the *koana* under the next loop of the middle warp strand to the left of the first insertion and pull it through until the loop is tight against the bracelet.

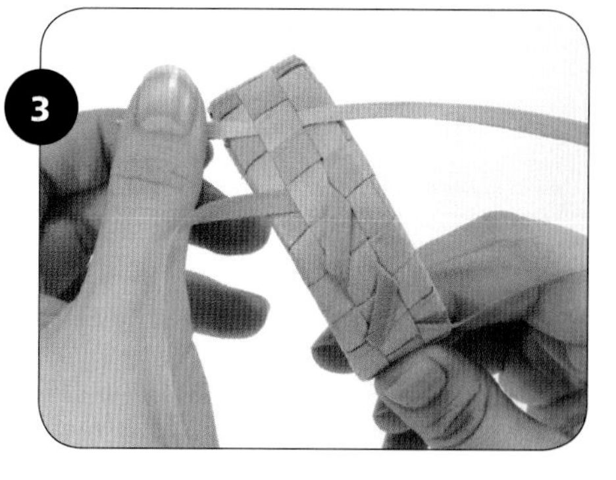


**3.** Continue this pattern until you reach the beginning of the bracelet.

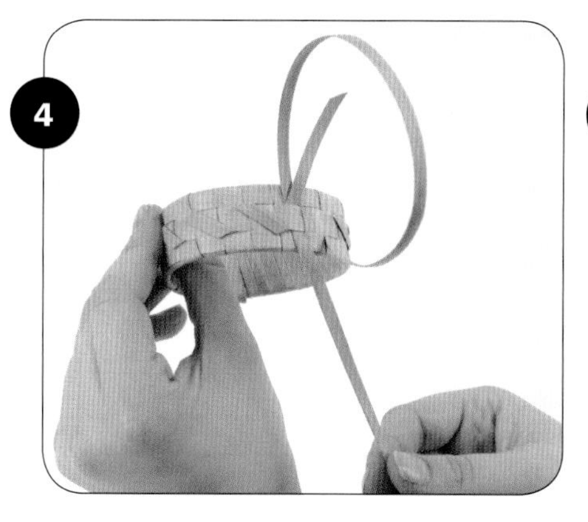


**4.** Insert the *koana* through the beginning stitch.

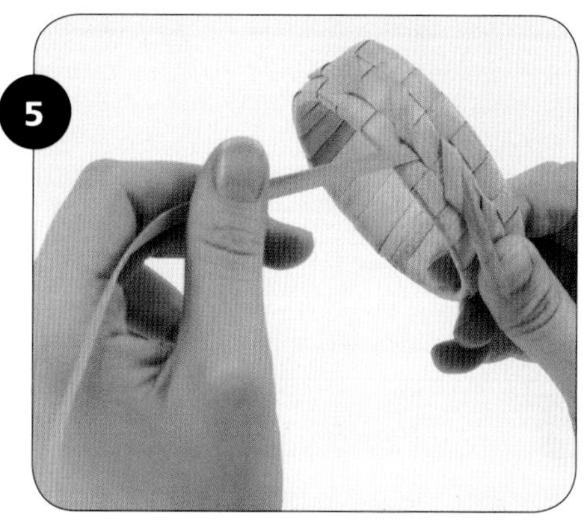


**5.** Pull the stitch tight. Make sure the tail piece is secured by this stitch.

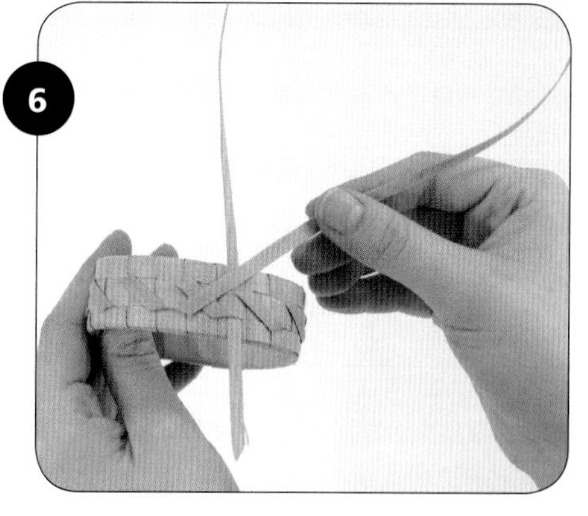


**6.** Reverse the direction of the stitch and insert the end of the weaving strand through the first loop, to the right, of the middle warp strand.

**7.** Continue the weaving pattern all the way around to the beginning, anchor the weaving strand and trim.

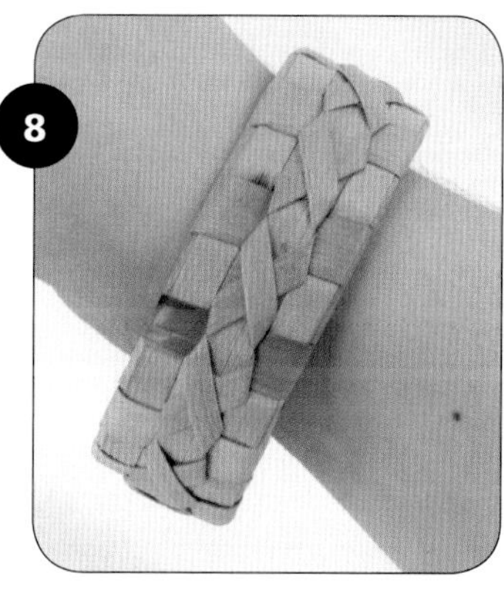


**8.** The finished embellishment.

# *Project 5:*
# Five-Warp-Strand Checkerboard #1
## 1/4-inch Wide Warp and 1/4-inch Wide Dark Wefts

**WHAT YOU'LL NEED:**

- 1/4-inch stripper, pins 2 squares apart

**PREPARATION:**

Make a bracelet coil that is 1-1/4 inch wide and strip the last 14 inches with the 1/4-inch stripper. This should produce five warp strands. Cut away any thin strips on either side after stripping.

**1.** Prepare a new strip of your darkest *lauhala* and using your 1/4-inch stripper, strip the leaf into 1/4-inch *koana*. You can also dye the prepared *lauhala* before stripping.

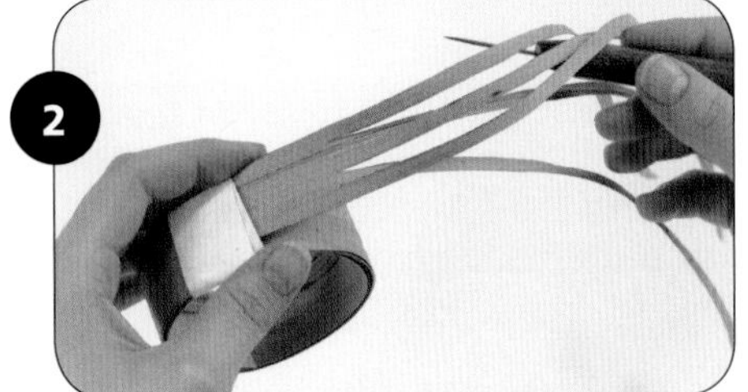

**2.** Hold your bracelet coil so that the five warp elements are horizontal and are to the right of the coil.

**3.** Use your awl to make a space between the individual plies of the coil adjacent to the masking tape and the loose warp strands. With the cuticle facing the center, slide the end of the 1/4-inch weft into the space between the plies. Allow 3/4-inch to extend beyond the coil.

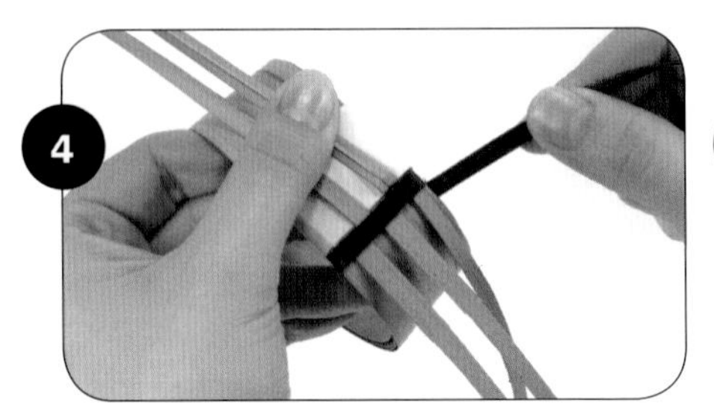

**4.** Row 1: Fold the second and fourth warp strands back on themselves. Lay the weft strand over the first, third and fifth warp strands and over the space occupied by the second and fourth warp strands.

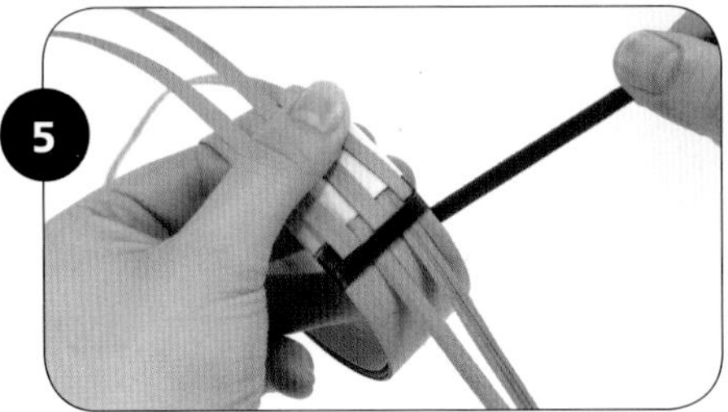

**5.** Row 2: Fold the first, third and fifth warp strands back on themselves. Lay the weft strand over the second and fourth warp strands and over the space occupied by the first, third and fifth warp strands.

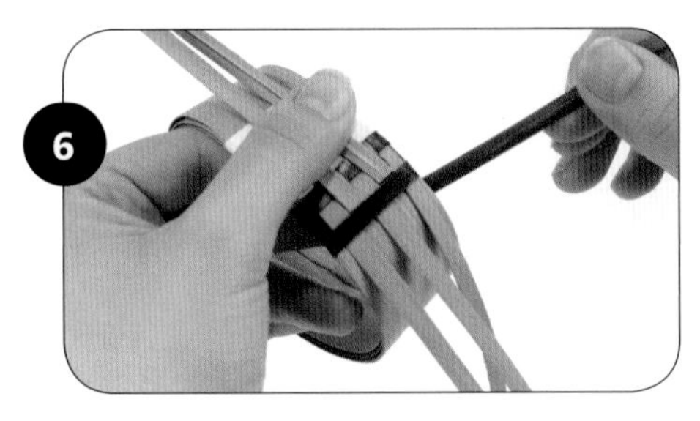

**6.** Row 3: Fold the second and fourth warp strands back on themselves. Lay the weft strand over the first, third and fifth warp strands and over the space occupied by the second and fourth warp strands.

**7.** Continue this pattern for the duration of the bracelet.

**8.** When all the weaving is finished, trim the ends of the *koana*.

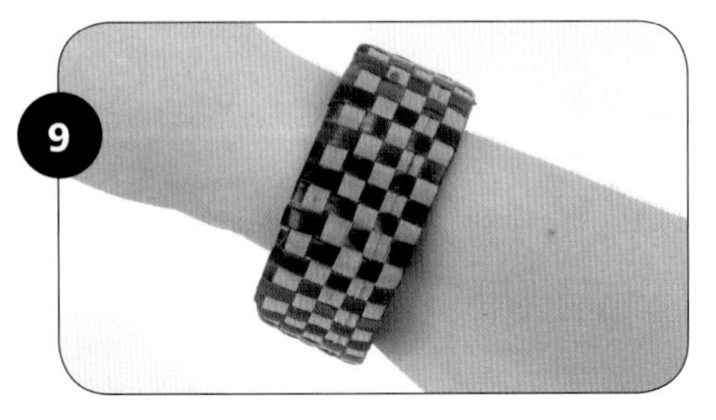

**9.** The completed checkerboard bracelet.

# *Project 6:* Five-Warp-Strand Checkerboard #2

## Four 1/4-inch and One 1/2-inch Warp Strands; 1/4-inch Weft Strands

**PREPARATION:**
Make a stripper for a bracelet coil 1-1/2 inch wide. Then strip the last 14 inches of the coil so that you have two outside warp strands which are 1/4-inch wide and a center warp strand 1/2-inch wide. Prepare a second *koana* 14 inches long and 1/2-inch wide in a darker color.

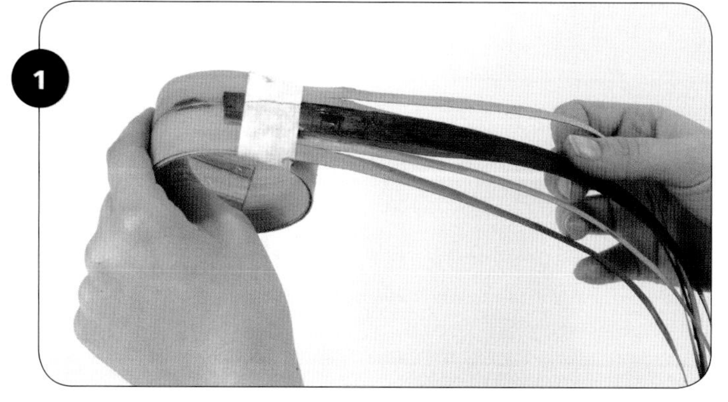

**1.** Hold your bracelet coil so that the five warp elements are horizontal and are to the right of the coil. Insert the darker, 14-inch strand over the middle warp strand and secure in place with the masking tape.

**2.** Row 1: Fold warp strands one, three, and five back on themselves. Lay the weaver over warp strands two and four.

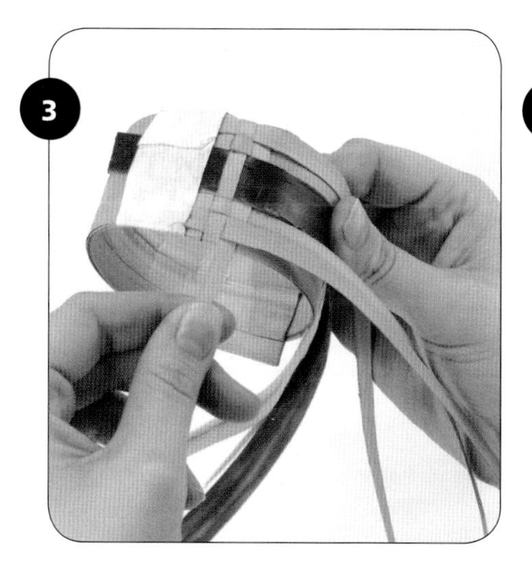

**3.** Lay warp strands one, three, and five over the weaver.

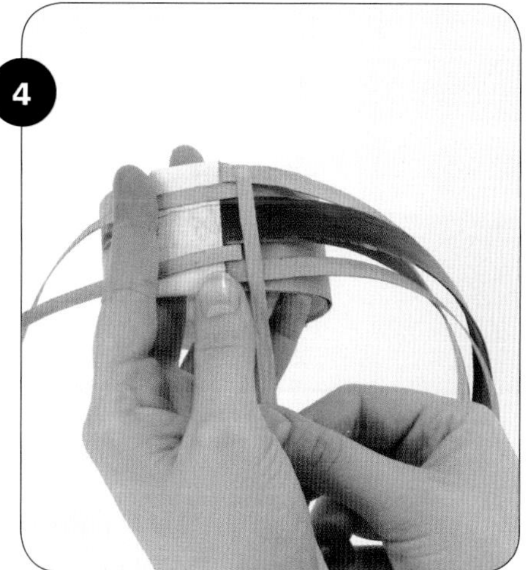

**4.** Row 2: Fold back warp strands two and four. Lay the weaving element over warp strands one, three and five.

**5.** Continue this pattern to the end of the bracelet.

# *Project 7:*
# Over 2 Under 2 Twill
## 1/4-inch Warps; 1/4-inch Wefts

**TIP:** *The trick for this bracelet is to see the pattern: Which strands are folded back for each row. We're always folding back two adjacent pairs (1 and 2, 2 and 3, 3 and 4, 4 and 5 or 5 and 1) plus the "odd" single strand occasionally. Once you recognize this pattern after several rows of weaving, the remainder of the bracelet pattern should be fairly easy to track.*

**PREPARATION:**
Strip a bracelet coil 1-1/4 inch wide. Strip the last 14 inches into five warp strands,1/4-inch wide each. Strip a dark *lauhala* into 1/4-inch wefts.

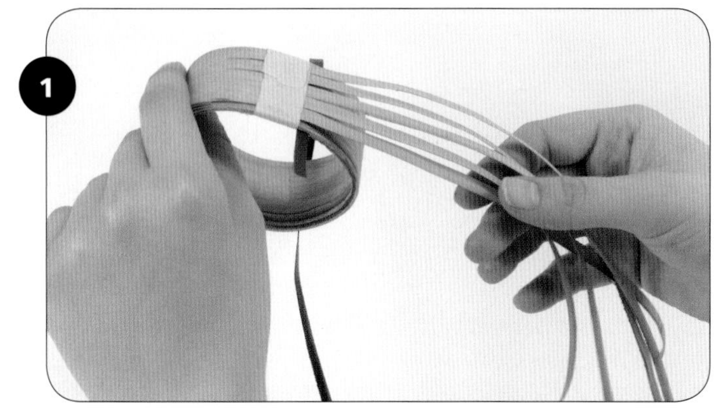

**1.** Hold your bracelet coil so that the five warp elements are horizontal and are to the right of the coil. With the cuticle facing the center, slide the end of the 1/4-inch weft into the space between the plies. Allow 3/4 inch to extend beyond the coil.

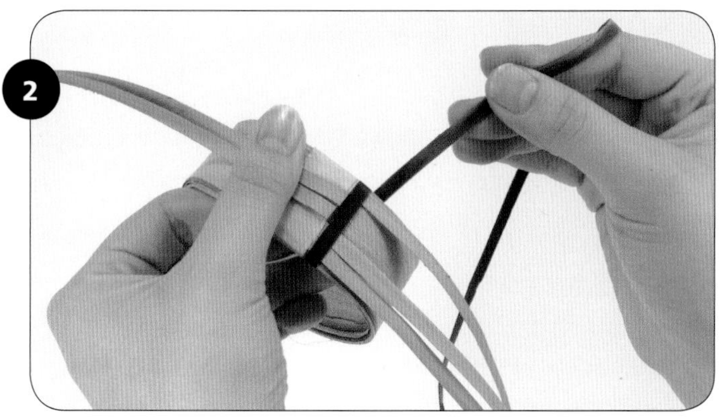

**2.** Row 1: Fold the second and third warp back on themselves and lay the weft on top of warp one, four and five.

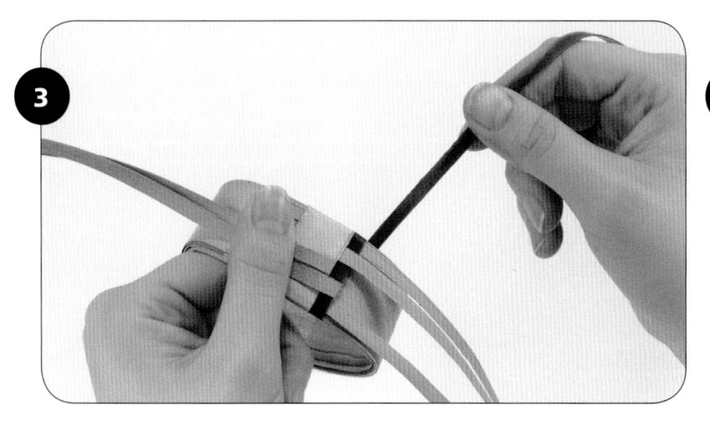

**3.** Row 2: Fold warp three and four back on themselves, lay the weft on top of warp one, two and five.

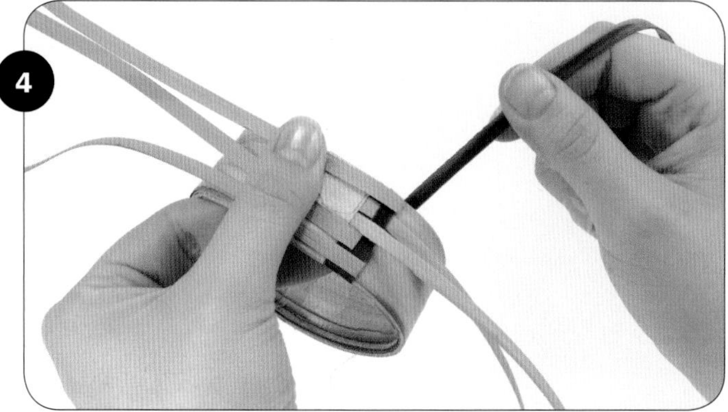

**4.** Row 3: Fold warp one, four and five back on themselves, lay the weft on top of warp two and three.

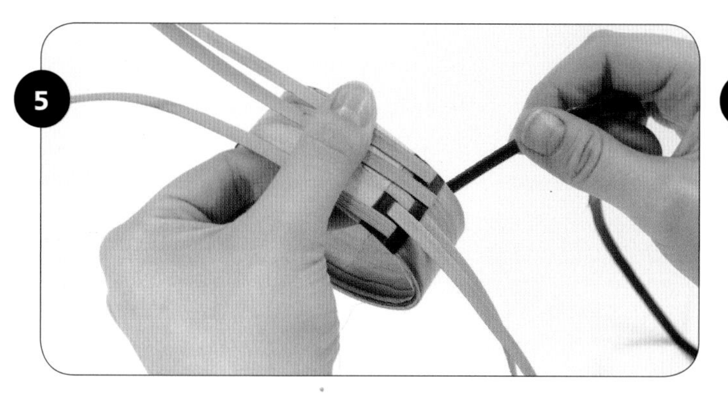

**5.** Row 4: Fold warp one, two and five back on themselves, lay the weaver on top of warp three and four.

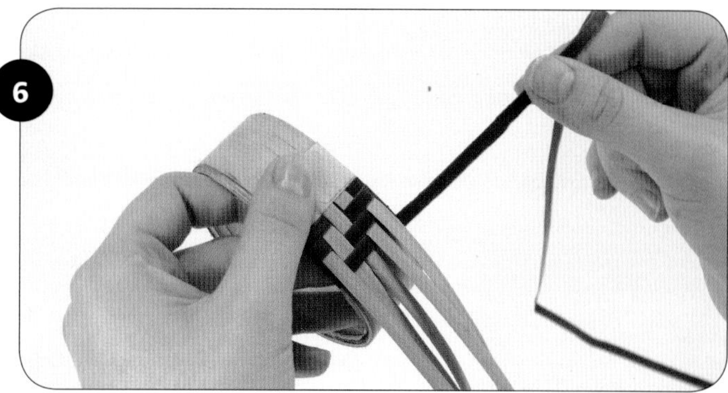

**6.** Row 4: Unfold all warp strands to check the emerging pattern in your work.

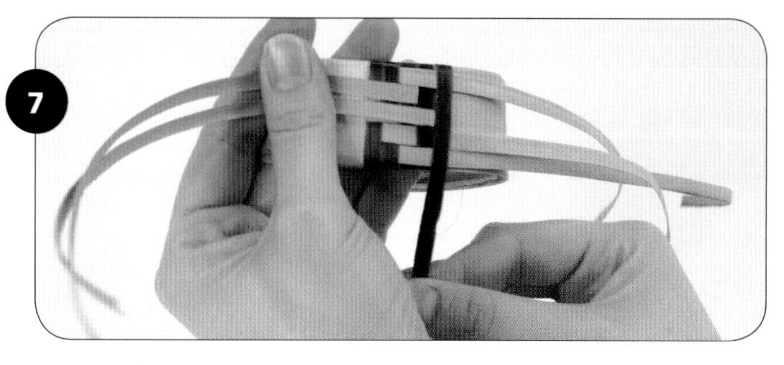

**7.** Row 5: Fold warp two and three back on themselves, lay the weaver over strands one, four and five This is identical to Row 1.

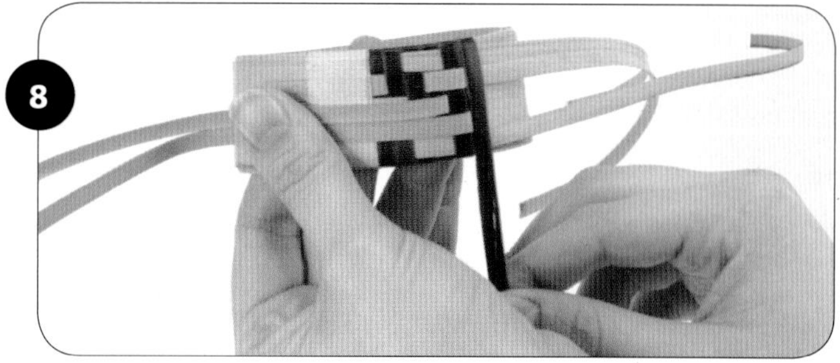

**8.** Row 6: Fold warp strands three and four back on themselves, lay the weaver over weavers one, two and five.

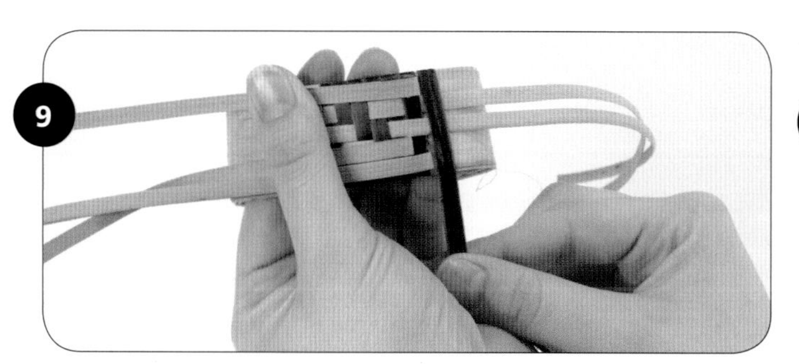

**9.** Row 7: Fold warp strands one, four and five back on themselves. Lay the weaver over warp strands two and three.

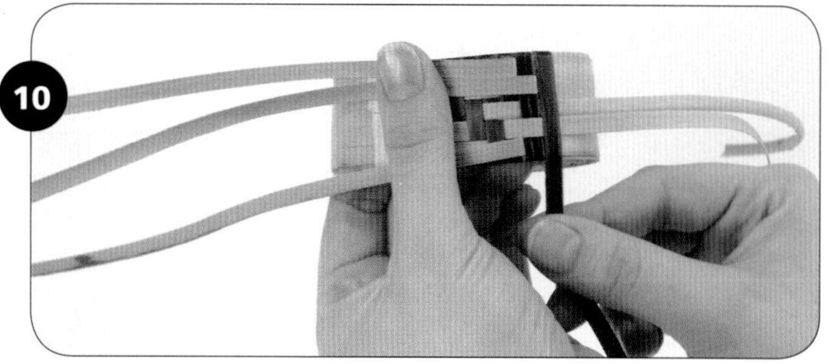

**10.** Row 8: Fold warp strands one, two and five back on themselves. Lay the weaver over warp strands three and four.

**11.** Row 9: Fold the warp strands two and three back on themselves and lay the weaver over warp strands one, four and five. This is identical to Row 1 and Row 5.

**12.** Continue weaving this pattern until you reach the beginning and Row 1. Interweave the warp strands into the first several rows and interweave the weft strand into Row 1. Trim the ends.

# *Project 8:*
# Reverse Twill
## 1/8-inch Warp Strands; 1/8-inch Weft Strands

**WHAT YOU'LL NEED:**

- 5/8-inch wide bracelet coil
- 16-inch dyed *lauhala*, with last 14 inches stripped into 1/8-inch *koana*
- 1/8-inch wefts, left natural

**PREPARATION:**

Tape the 2-inch head of the dyed *lauhala* to the bracelet coil.

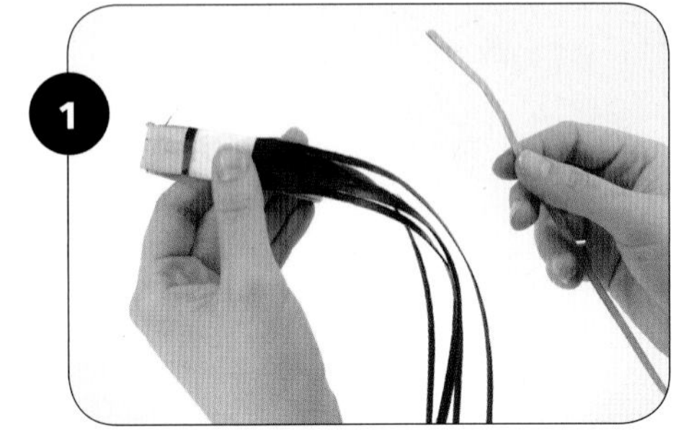

**1.** Hold the wrist band with the five dyed warp strands facing to the right. The weft *koana* are also 1/8-inch wide.

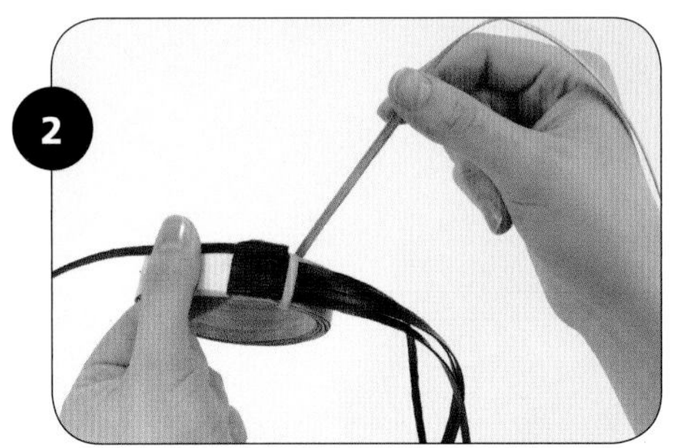

**2.** Row 1: Fold back warp strand 1. Weave over warp strands 2, 3, 4 and 5.

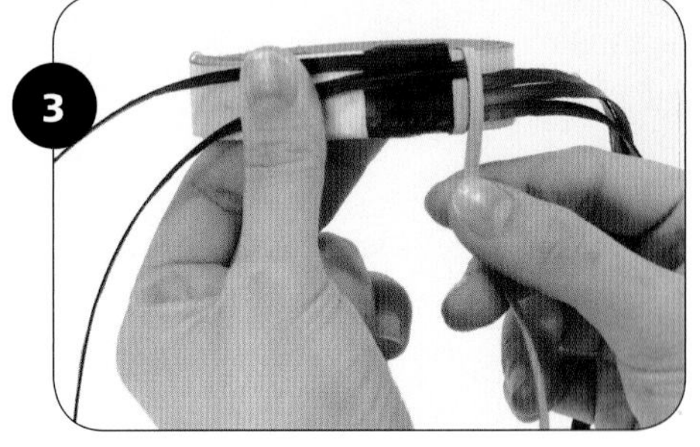

**3.** Row 2: Fold back warp strands 1 and 2. Weave over warp strands 3, 4 and 5.

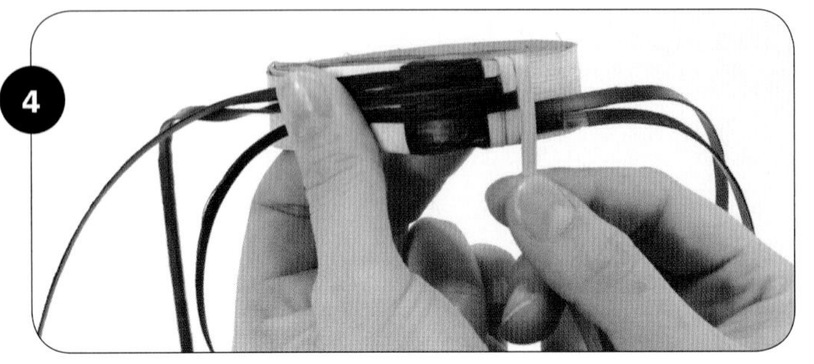

**4.** Row 3: Fold back warp strand 1, 2 and 3. Weave over 4 and 5.

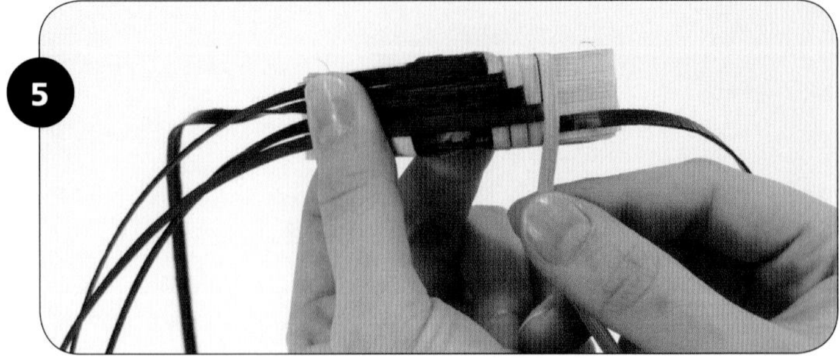

**5.** Row 4: Fold back warp strand 1, 2, 3 and 4. Weave over 5.

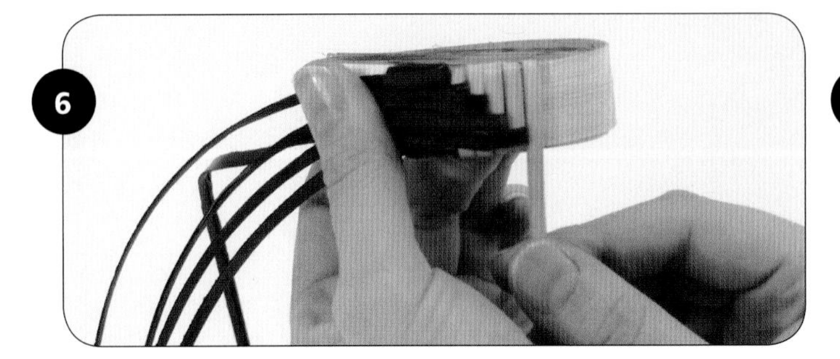

**6.** Row 5: Fold back warp strand 1, 2, 3, 4 and 5. Weave over the band.

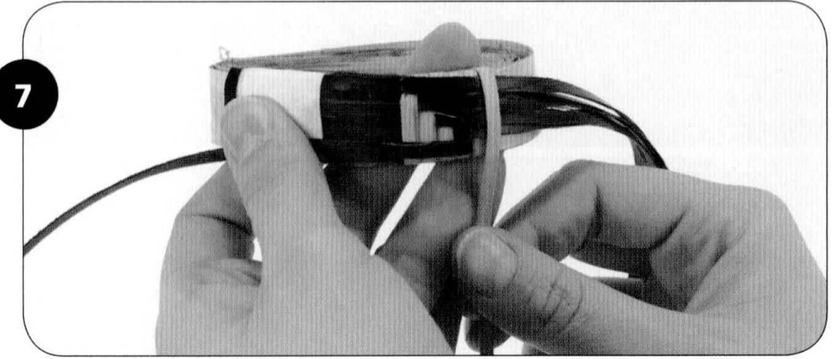

**7.** Row 6: Fold back warp strand 5. Weave over 1, 2, 3 and 4.

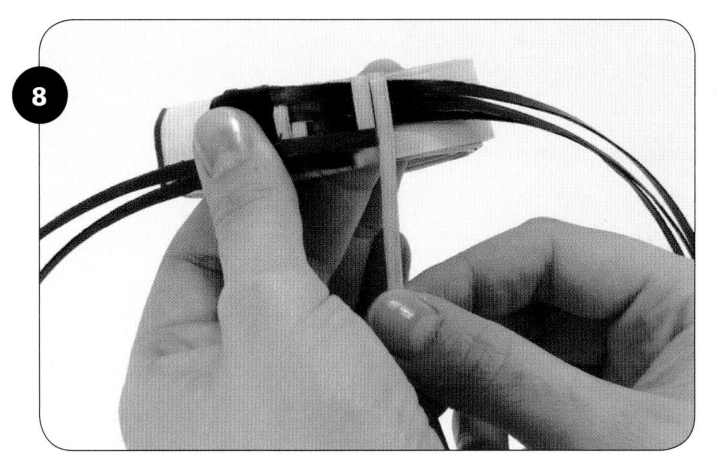

**8.** Row 7: Fold back warp strands 4 and 5. Weave over 1, 2 and 3.

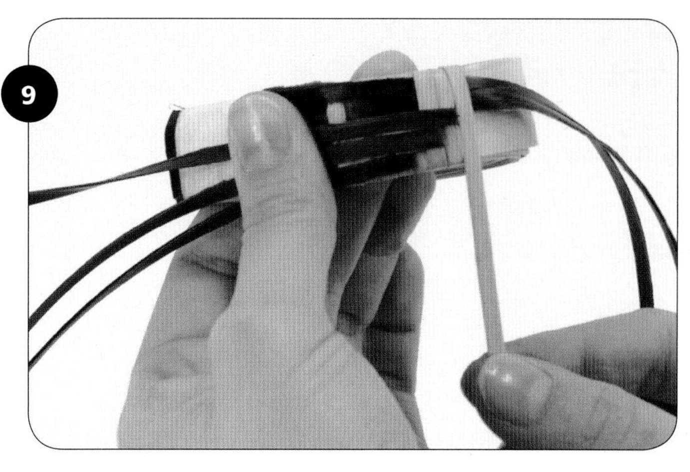

**9.** Row 8: Fold back warp strands 3, 4 and 5. Weave over 1 and 2.

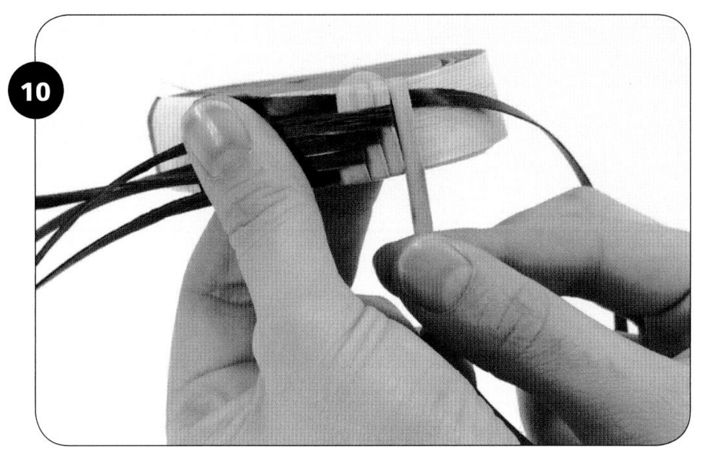

**10.** Row 9: Fold back war strands 2, 3, 4 and 5. Weave over 1.

**11.** Row 10: Fold back all warp strands. Weave over the band.

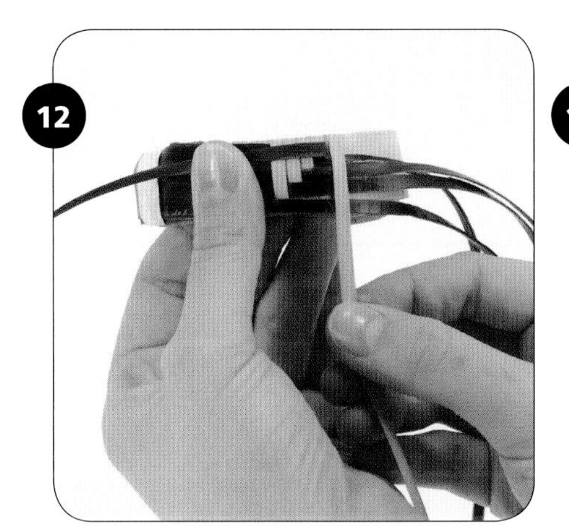

**12.** Row 11: Fold back warp strand 1. Weave over 2, 3, 4 and 5. Same as Row 1.

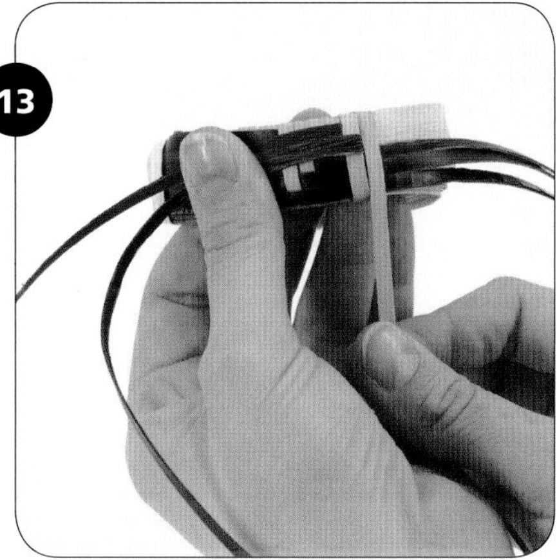

**13.** Row 12: Fold back warp strand 1 and 2. Weave over 3, 4 and 5. Same as Row 2.

**14.** Continue the pattern. When you reach the masking tape at the beginning of the band, remove it, and continue with the pattern interweaving the strands at the end.

# *Project 9:*
# Bracelet with Hole-Punch Warp and Bright-Color Embellishments

**WHAT YOU'LL NEED:**

- 1-1/8-inch wide bracelet foundation coil
- 3/8-inch wide warp strands
- 5/16-inch to 11/32-inch wide weft strand. (A full 3/8-inch width will make it difficult to keep the holes in the center of each stitch.)
- a paper or leather punch, 1/8-inch to 3/16-inch in diameter

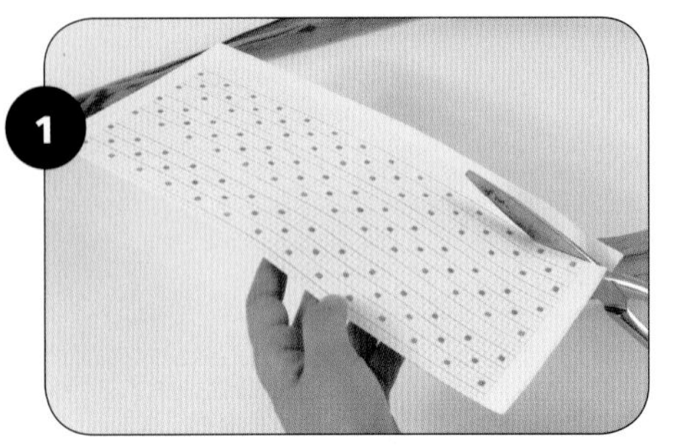

**1.** Photocopy the template pattern for Project 9 (see page 67) onto a sheet of sticky backed paper or a full sheet label. Carefully cut out a three row pattern. The template will be 1-1/8 inch wide by 10-1/2 inches long.

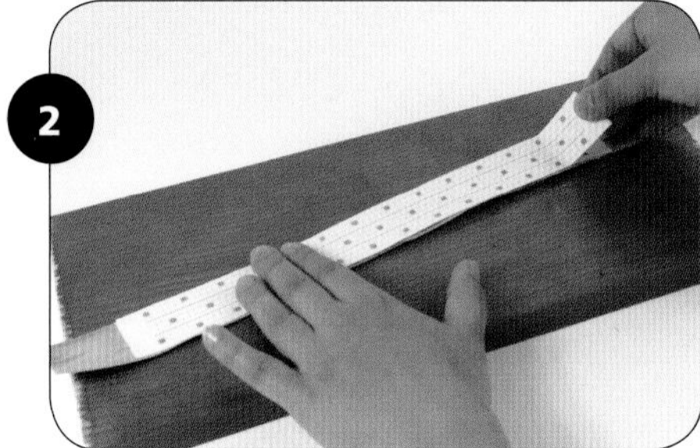

**2.** Cut and prepare a foundation strip 1-1/8 inch wide and 16-inches long. Remove the sticky back from the template and attach the template to the "wrong side" of the strip of *lauhala*.

**3.** Using a 1/4-inch or a 3/16-inch hole punch or leather punch, pierce through the template and leaf where the dots are on the template. Strip the template and leaf into three 3/8-inch warp strands still attached on the left side.

**4.** Lay the perforated template and *lauhala* combination on top of a length of colorful wrapping paper (mylar or hologram coated), and trim the paper to the same width.

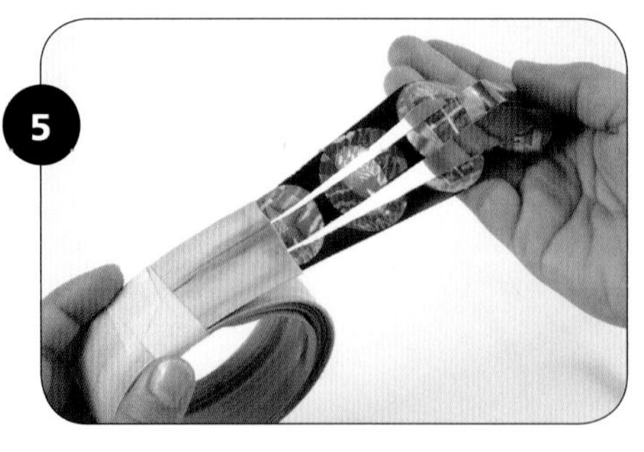

**5.** Strip the wrapping paper into three 3/8-inch warp strands, still attached on the left side. Slip the solid end of the wrapping paper warp strands into the bracelet foundation.

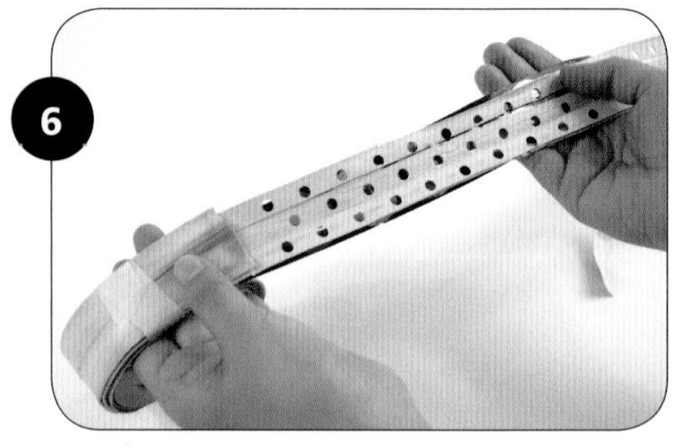

**6.** Slip the solid end of the *lauhala* combination on top of the wrapping paper warp and into the bracelet foundation. The good side of the *lauhala* should be up. The template side will be hidden in the weave.

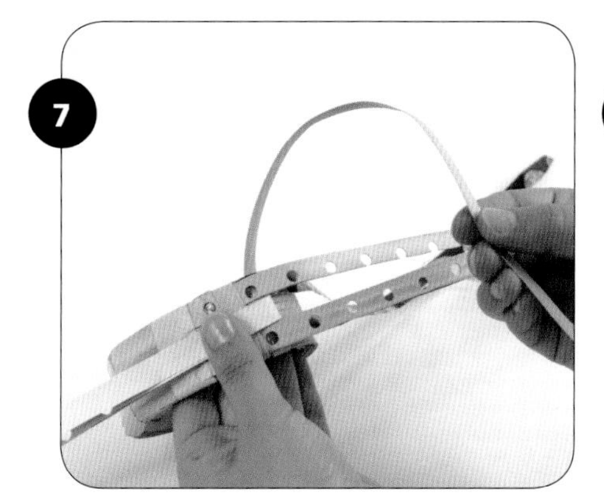

**7.** Using a 5/16-inch weft strand, weave under the first warp strand, over the second warp strand and under the third warp strand. Make sure the weaver is directly under the holes in the first and third warp strands. Bring the weaver through the center of the bracelet. Fold the middle warp strand back against itself and bring the weaver down over the first and third strands in the space between the punched holes.

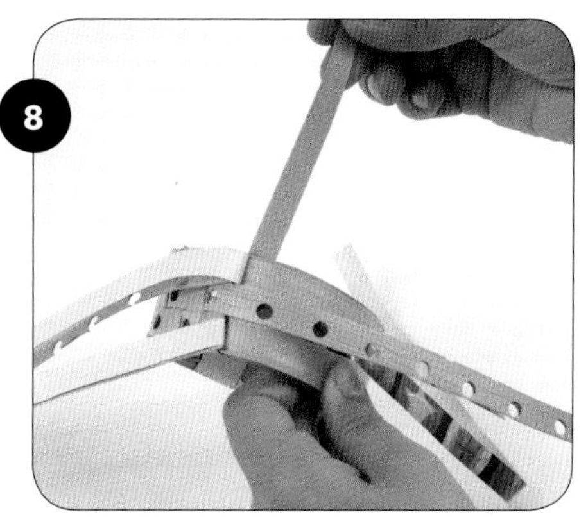

**8.** Fold the middle warp strand down on top of the weaver and then fold the first and third warp strands back against themselves to make the space for the weaving strand. Bring the weaver over the middle warp strand in the spot between two punched holes. Then fold the first and third strands down on top of the weaver and fold the middle strand back on itself. Continue the weaving pattern all the way around the bracelet.

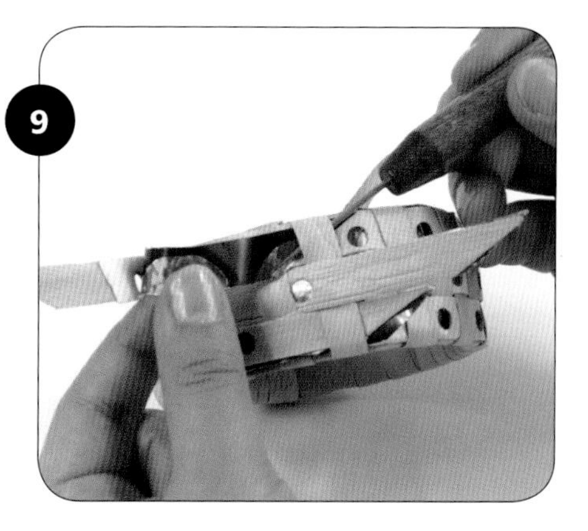

**9.** Use an awl to help interweave the ends of the warp strands (both leaf and paper) back into the beginning of the weave.

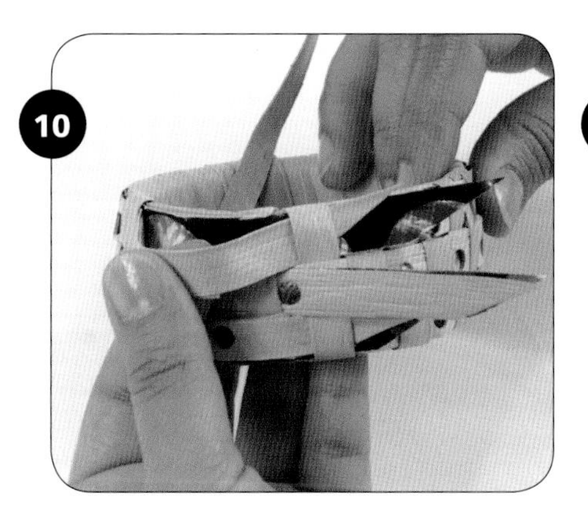

**10.** Pull the wrapping paper through first, then the *lauhala*.

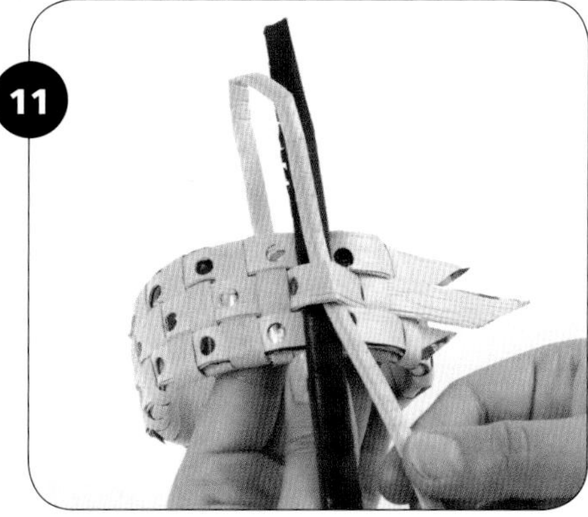

**11.** After the warp strands are interwoven, interweave the weft strand through the weave. Use a short length of *lauhala* (black in the photo) to hold a space for the weaver to slide through.

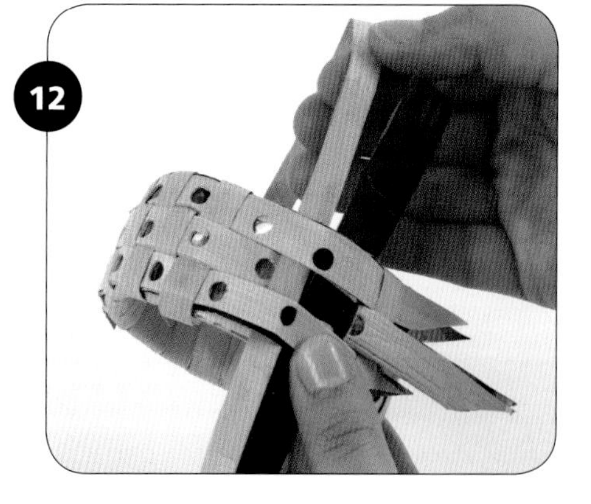

**12.** The final weave will be under the first and third warp strand so that the end is held in place at two anchor points. The black strip of leaf holds the weaving spot open. Pull all of the strand ends taut then trim.

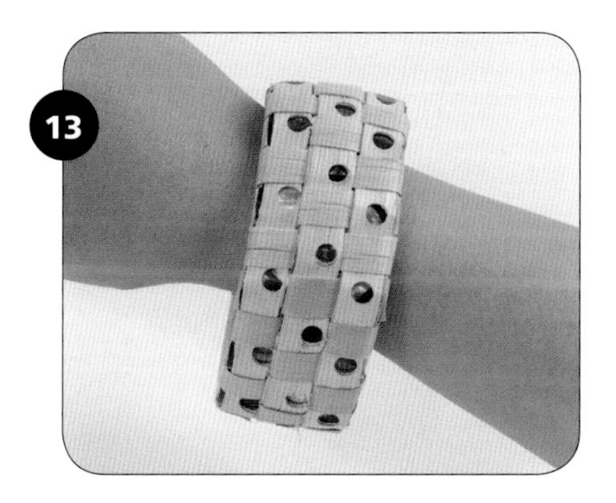

**13.** The finished bracelet.

*Project 10:*

# Domed Bracelet with Pattern

## How to Build a Dome

**BRACELET PATTERN:**

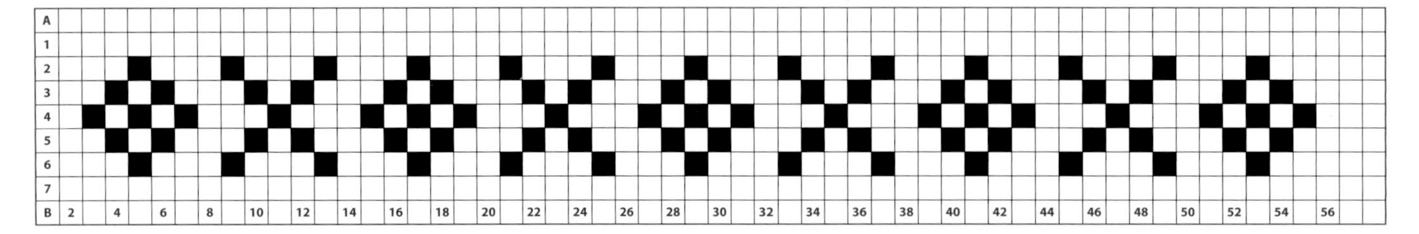

**1.** Strip three bracelet bands: 1-inch wide, 3/4-inch wide and 1/2-inch wide.

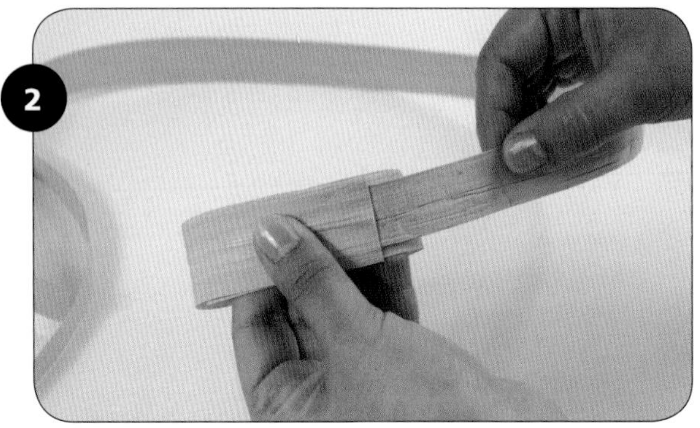

**2.** Make the first band from the 1-inch wide *koana*. Add in the beginning of the 3/4-inch *koana*.

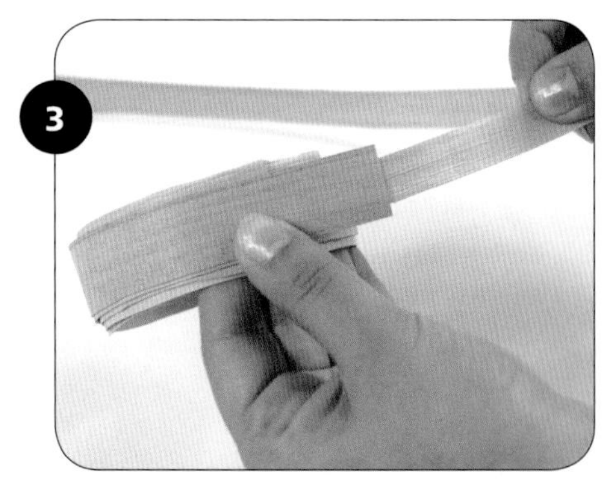

**3.** Add in the 1/2-inch *koana*. Adjust the band so that each successive layer is in the middle of the band.

**4.** Cut a *koana* 1-1/8-inch wide and 16 inches long from a dark color *lauhala* and strip all but the first 2 inches into nine 1/8-inch wide warp strands.

**5.** Row 1 and 2: Wrap over A, 1, 2, 3, 4, 5, 6, 7 and B.

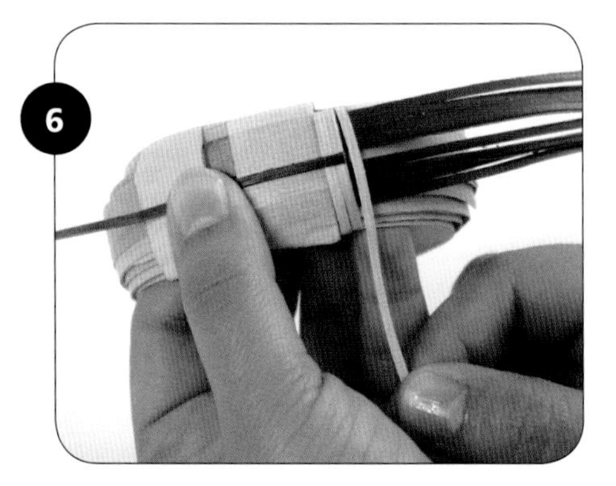

**6.** Row 3: Weave over A, 1, 2, 3, under 4, over 5, 6, 7 and B.

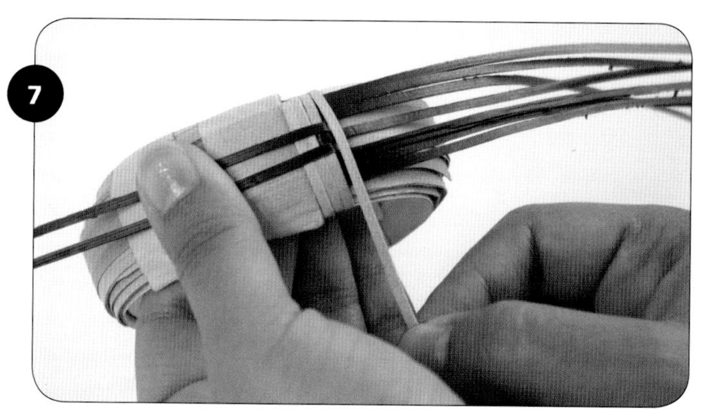


**7.** Row 4: Weave over A, 1, 2, under 3, over 4, under 5, over 6, 7 and B.

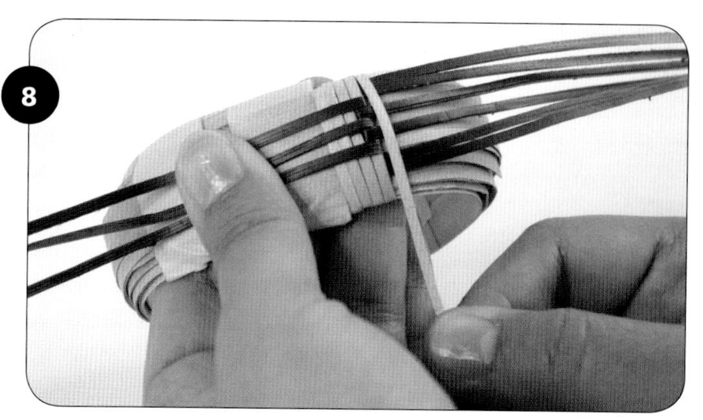


**8.** Row 5: Weave over A, under 2, over 3, under 4, over 5, under 6, over 7 and B.

**9.** Row 6: Weave over A, 1, 2 under 3, over 4, under 5, over 6, 7 and B.

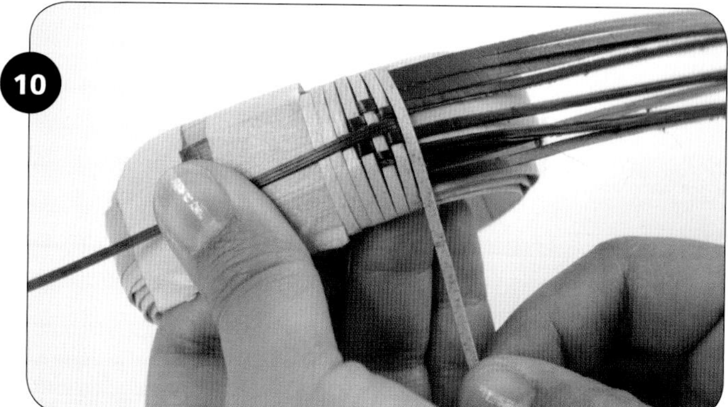


**10.** Row 7: Weave over A, 1, 2, 3 under 4, over 5, 6, 7 and B.

**11.** Row 8: Wrap over A, 1, 2, 3, 4, 5, 6, 7 and B.

**12.** Row 9 : Weave over A, 1, under 2, over 3, 4, 5, under 6, over 7 and B.

**13:** Row 10: Weave over A, 1, 2, under 3, over 4, under 5, over 6, 7 and B.

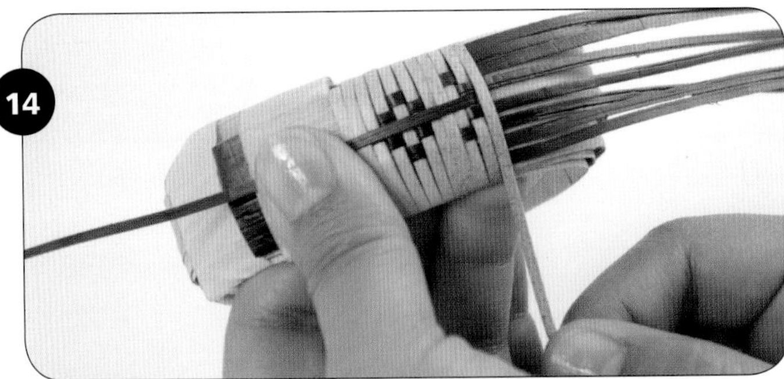

**14:** Row 11: Weave over A, 1, 2, 3, under 4, over 5, 6, 7 and B.

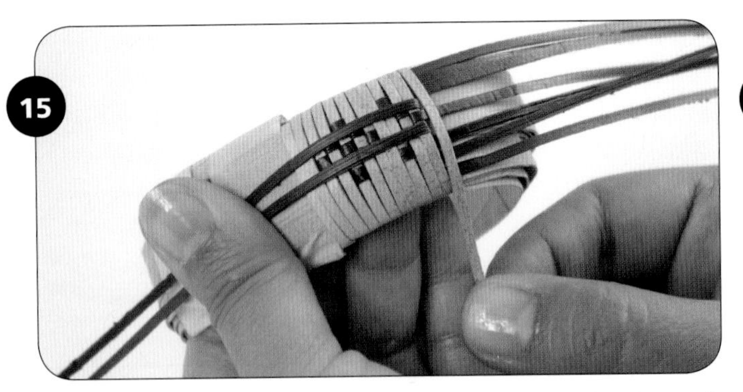

**15:** Row 12: Weave over A, 1, 2, under 3, over 4, under 5, over 6, 7 and B.

**16.** Row 13 Weave over A, 1, under 2, over 3, 4, 5, under 6, over 7 and B.

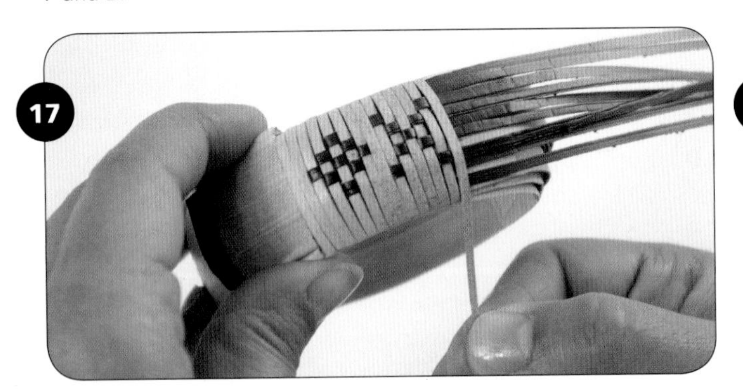

**17:** Row 14: Wrap over all.

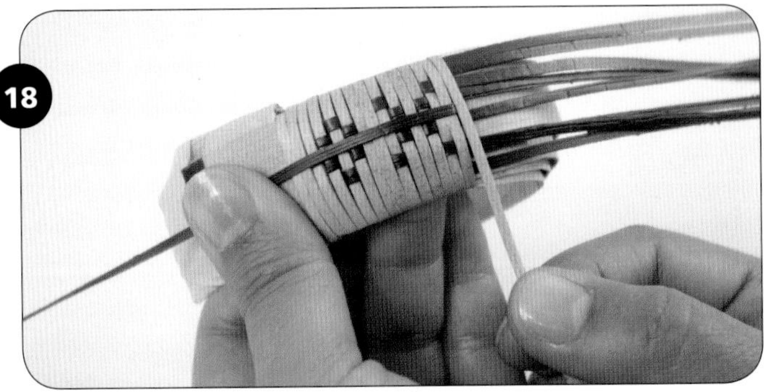

**18.** Row 15: Weave over A, 1, 2, 3, under 4, over 5, 6, 7 and B. This is the same as Row 3 and the beginning of the pattern.

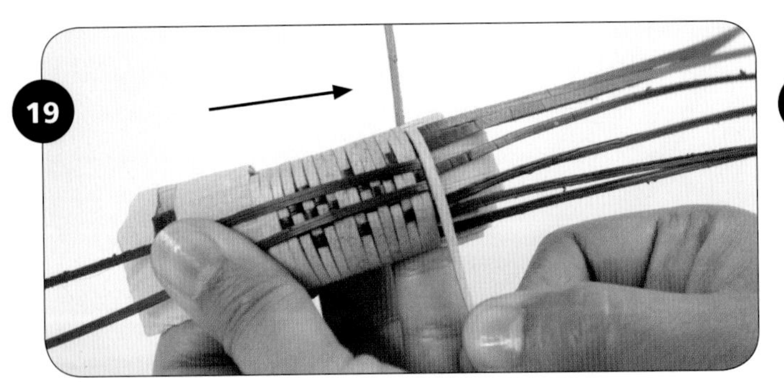

**19.** Row 16: Same as Row 4, but here we are going to splice in a new weft. Insert it between the layers of the foundation on the top side of the bracelet and weave over A, 1, 2,under 3, over 4, under 5, over 6, 7 and B. The old wrapping strand is pointing up (arrow).

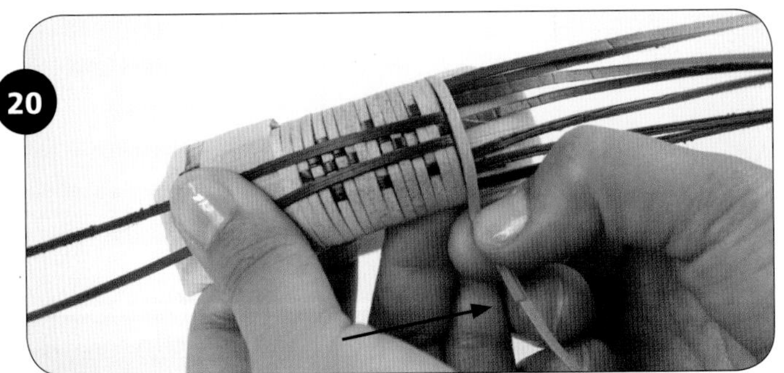

**20.** Lay the old weaver (arrow) over the new strand.

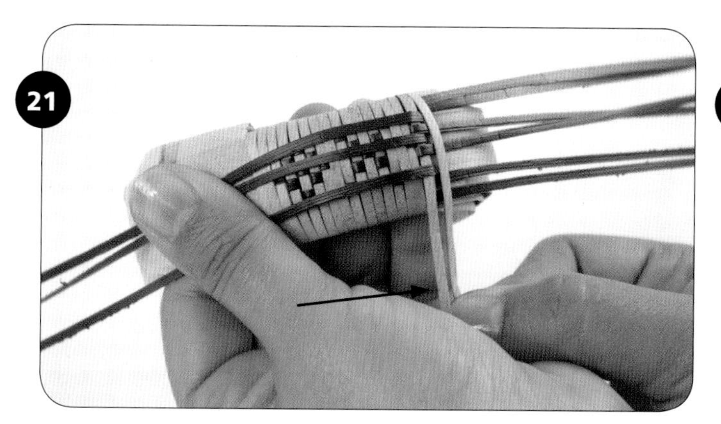

**21.** Row 17: Weave the new strand over A and 1, under 2, over 3, under 4, over 5, under 6, over 7 and B. Leave the old weft (arrow) alone.

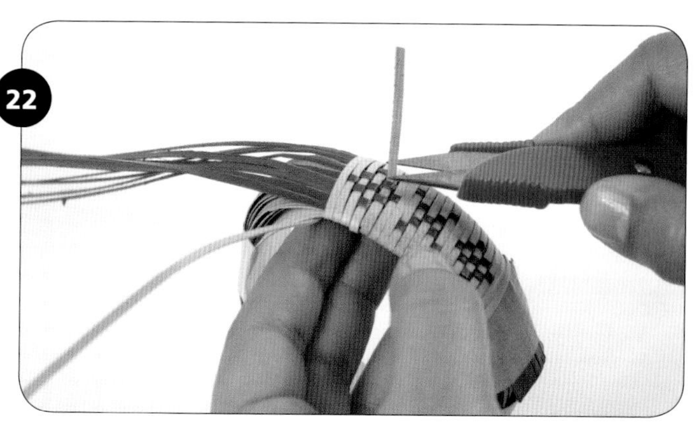

**22.** Trim the old weft after the weaving has continued a few more rows.

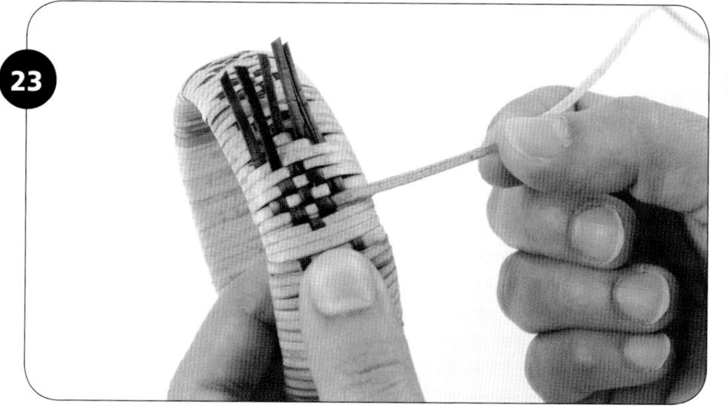

**23.** When you reach the beginning of the weaving, interweave the warp strands back into the weave as well as the wrapping strand.

**24.** Make sure the wrapping strand is secured by at least two warps, then trim as close as possible.

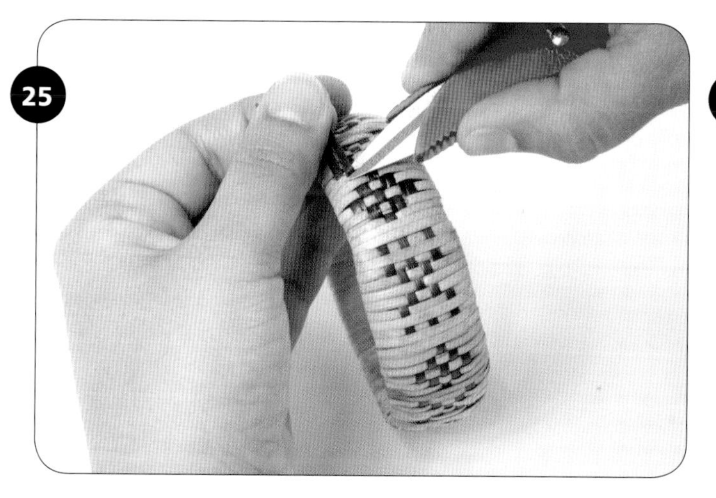

**25.** Moisten the strand with a spray bottle or wet cloth, give it a little pull and cut while it is under a little tension. The cut strand will pull back under the weft.

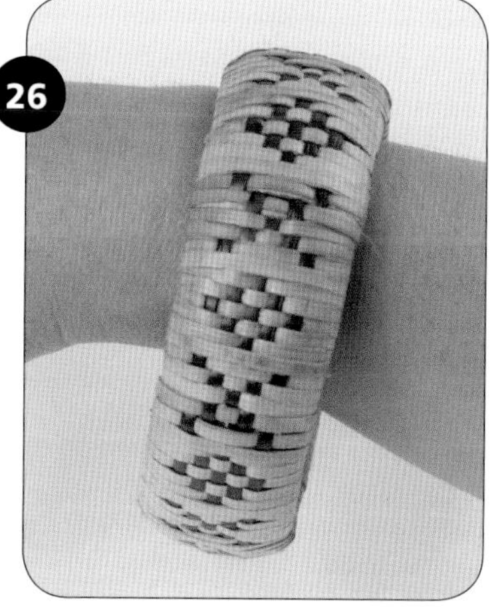

**26.** The finished bracelet.

# *Project 11:* Pinwheel Embellishment

## Stars Woven Over 2 Warp Elements

**WHAT YOU'LL NEED:**

- Two-Warp or Six-Warp Checkerboard Bracelet
- *koana*, dyed and stripped to same width as warp strands

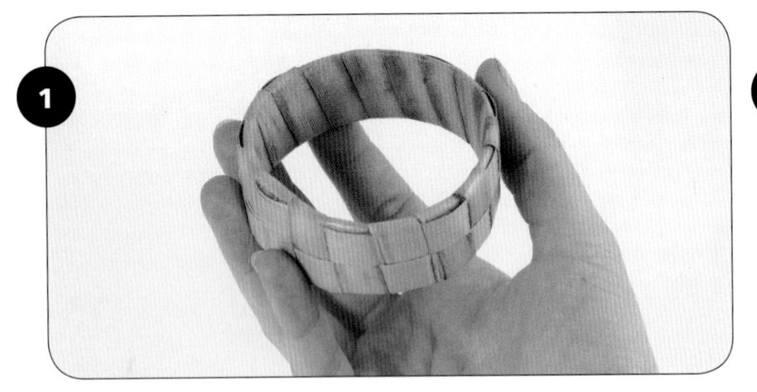

**1.** Weave a 2-warp or a 6-warp checkerboard band. We'll use both warps in the 2-warp band or the middle two warp strands in the 6-warp band.

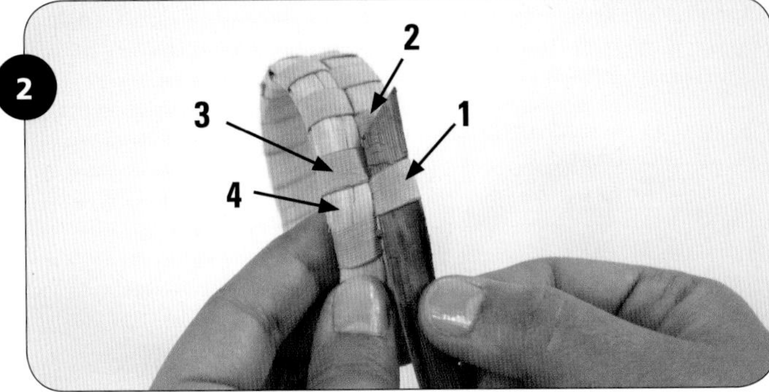


**2.** There are many ways to weave the "star" or "pinwheel" pattern, we'll just show one version. Insert the *koana*, cuticle side down, under Loop 1 from the bottom, on the lower warp strand.

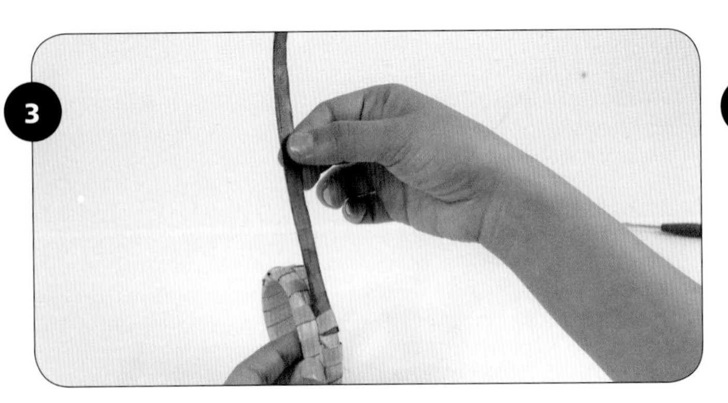

**3.** Pull the strand all the way up until the bottom edge of the strand is flush with the bottom of Loop 1.

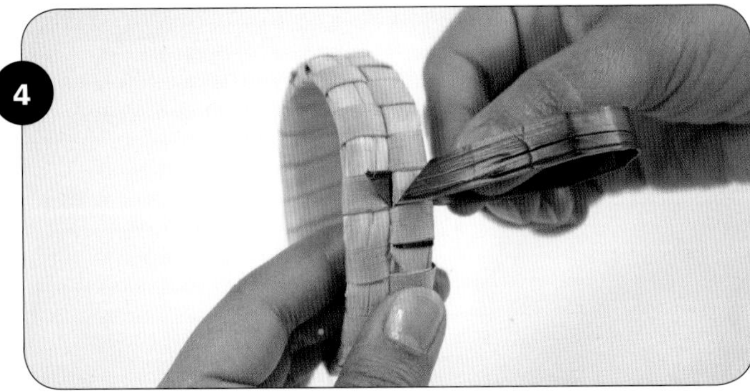

**4.** Fold the *koana* at a 90 degree angle facing right. The cuticle side will show. Tuck the tip of the weave back through Loop 2.

**5.** Pull left until the *koana* forms an even and taut fold covering half of Loop 2.

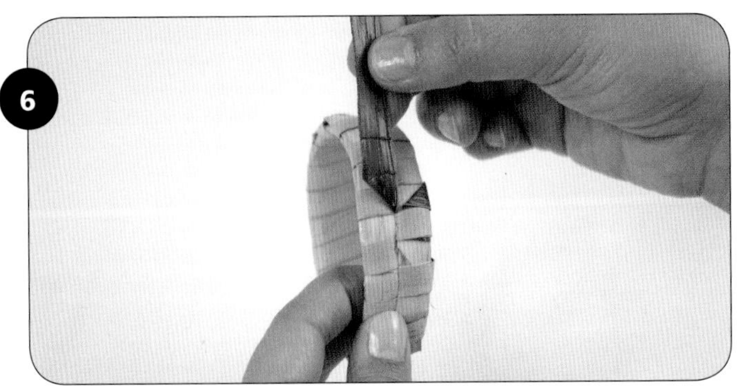

**6.** Fold the *koana* at a 90 degree angle facing up. The cuticle side will show.

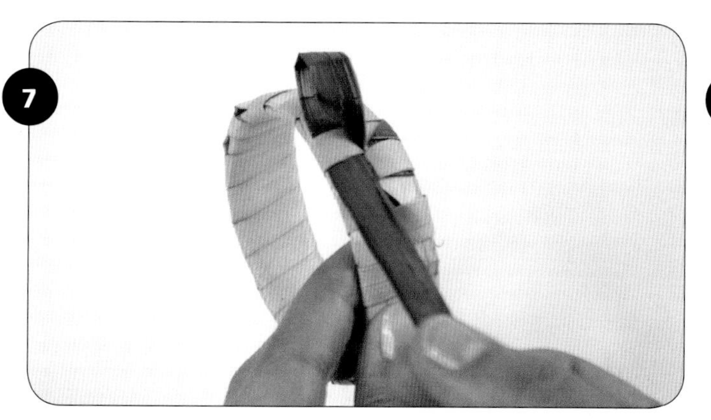


**7.** Fold back and insert the *koana* into Loop 3 from the top and pull down until the *koana* forms an even and taut fold covering half of Loop 3.

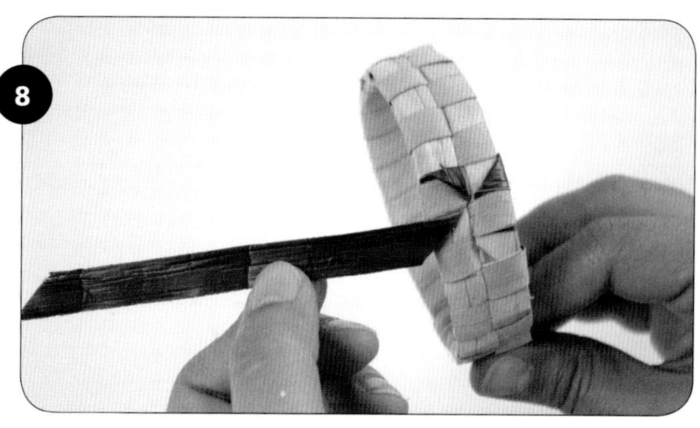


**8.** Fold the *koana* at a 90 degree angle facing left. The cuticle side will show.

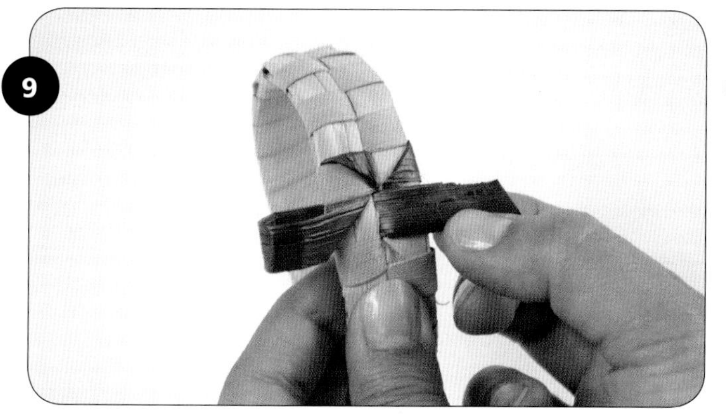


**9.** Fold back and insert the *koana* into Loop 4 from the left and pull right until the *koana* forms an even and taut fold covering half of Loop 4.

**10.** Fold the *koana* at a 90 degree angle facing down. The cuticle side will show.

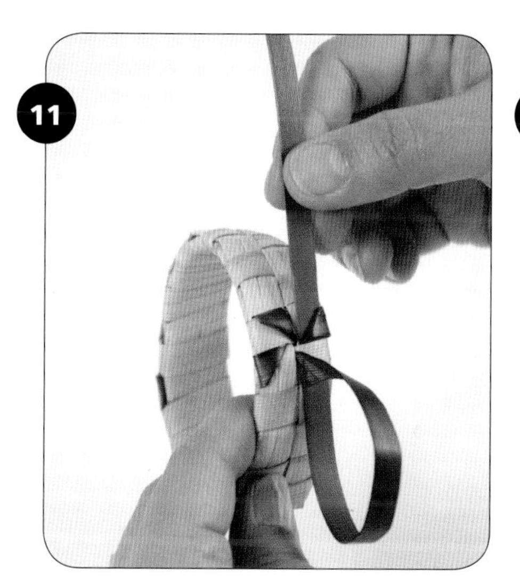


**11.** Fold the *koana* at a 90 degree angle facing up and insert the *koana* back into Loop 1 and under the first stitch. Be careful not to loosen the first stitch.

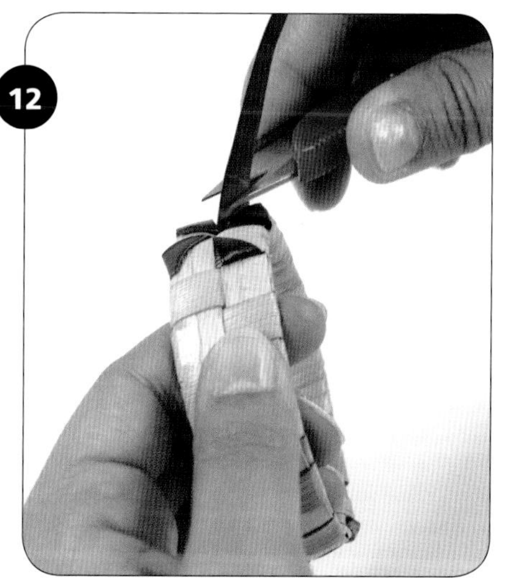


**12.** Trim the ends and begin again.

**13.** Continue in this manner until you finish weaving the bracelet.

# *Project 12:* Single Curl Embellishment

**WHAT YOU'LL NEED:**

- Project 1 bracelet
- *koana*, dyed and stripped to same width as weft strands

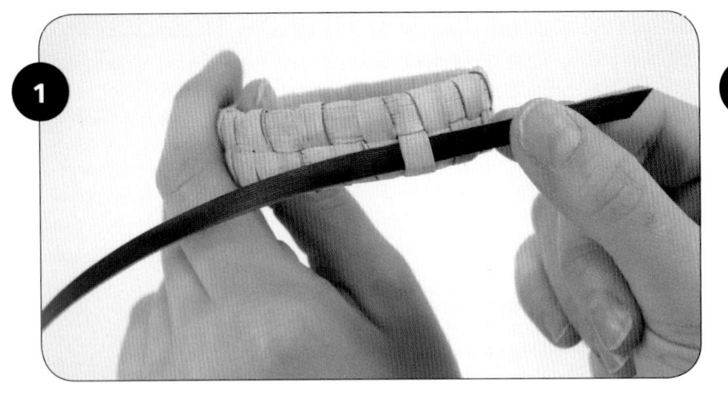

**1.** Insert the *koana* from left to right, with the cuticle down, under a loop in the lower row.

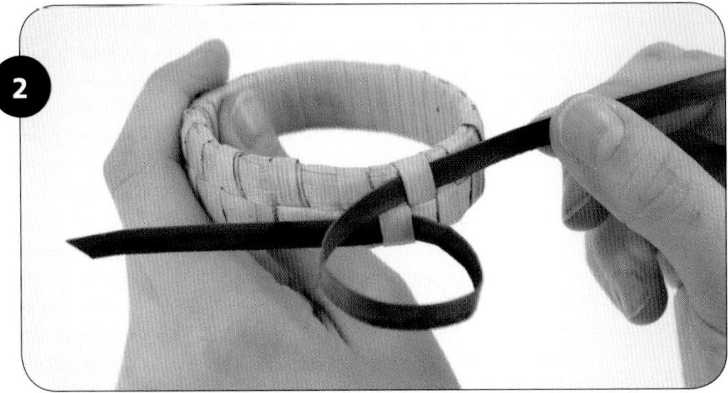

**2.** With the cuticle side down, insert the *koana* under the adjacent loop in the upper row.

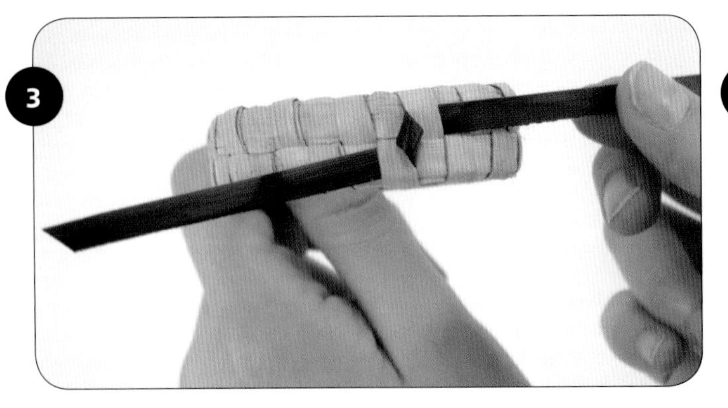

**3.** Slowly pull the loop in the *koana* strand taut. The cuticle side should be up and showing.

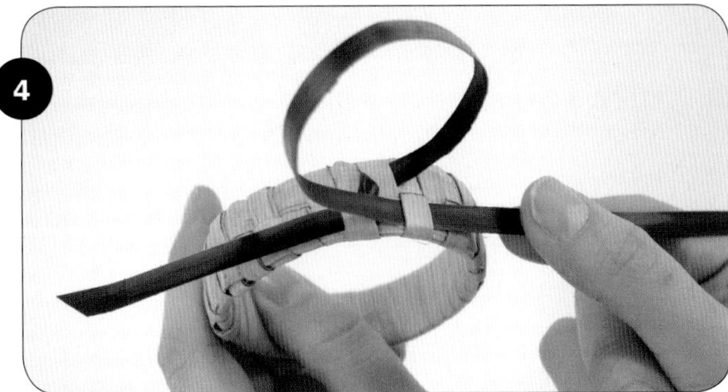

**4.** With the cuticle side down, insert the *koana* under the adjacent loop in the lower row.

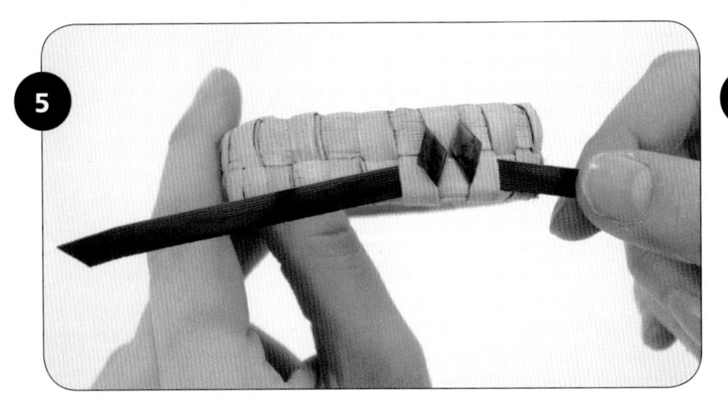

**5.** Slowly pull the loop in the *koana* taut. The cuticle side should be up and showing.

**6.** Continue this pattern all the way around the bracelet.

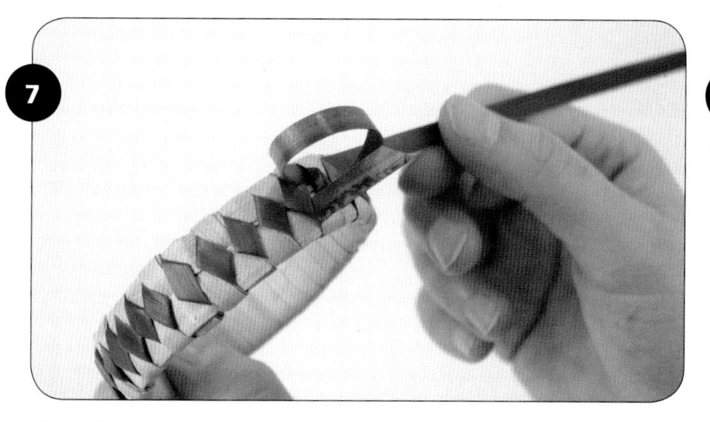

**7-8.** Finish by overlapping one or two curls.

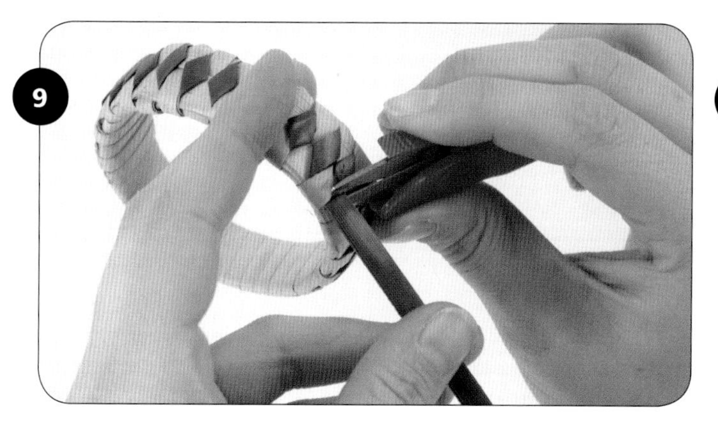

**9.** Trim the ends when you have finished with the overlap.

**10.** The finished bracelet.Try for uniformity of the curls and pull them taut enough to flatten the loop, but not so taut that they disappear into the weaving.

# Project 13:
# Double Curl Embellishment
## With Variations

**WHAT YOU'LL NEED:**
- Two-Warp Checkerboard Bracelet (page 23)
- *koana* of same width

**1.** The first row of curls is woven as in the Single Curl Embellishment (page 46), but using the lower and middle warp strands.

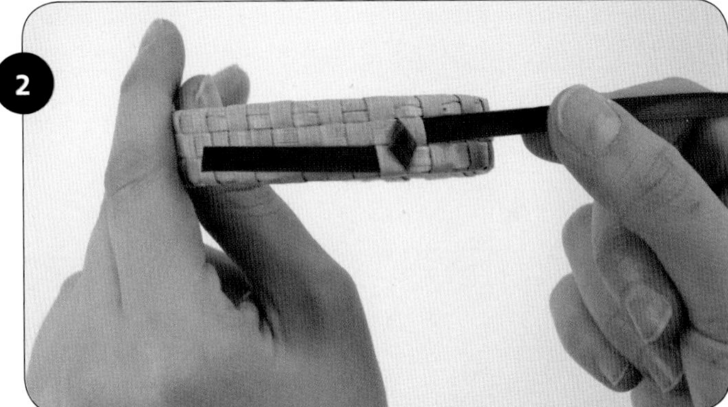

**2.** Pull the curl taut, making sure the cuticle side is turned up. Leave room for another insertion in the middle warp column for the second curl. Weave the single curl all the way around the band as in the previous project.

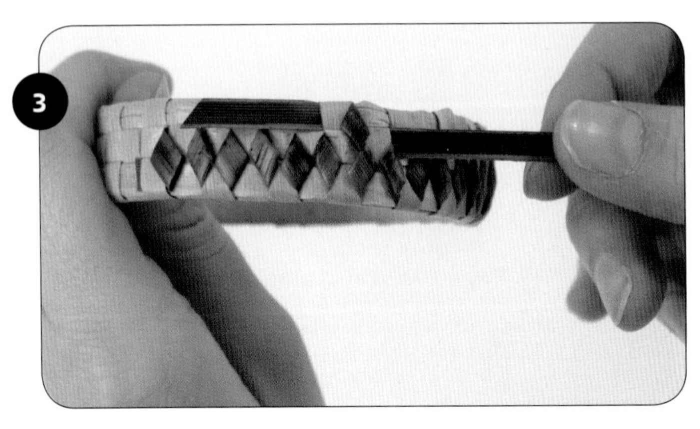

**3.** Begin the second row of curls with the upper and middle warp strands. Bring the *koana* under the loop on the upper warp and back through the adjacent middle loop. Pull taut. (One curl has been completed in the photo above.

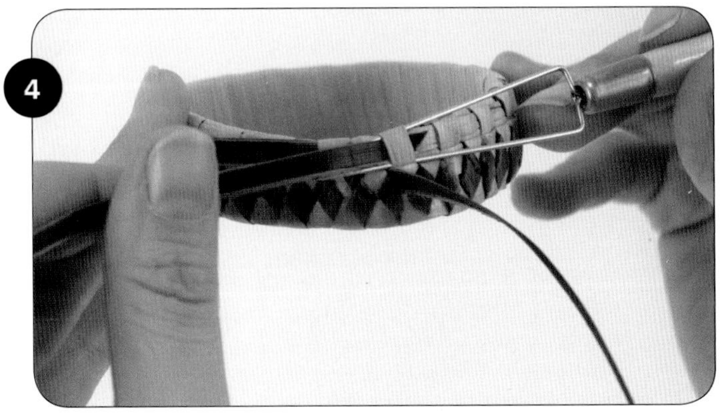

**4.** If needed, use a wire loop tool or an awl to make a space to insert the weaver under the adjacent loop to the right with the upper warp strand.

**5.** Pull the loop taut as in the previous steps.

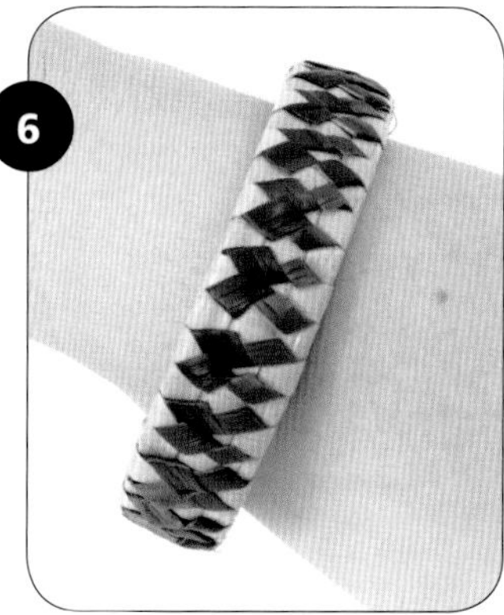

**6.** Continue weaving the pattern around the bracelet.

**7.** Variation: wide middle band and double curls.

Variation: little points on the end of each single curl.

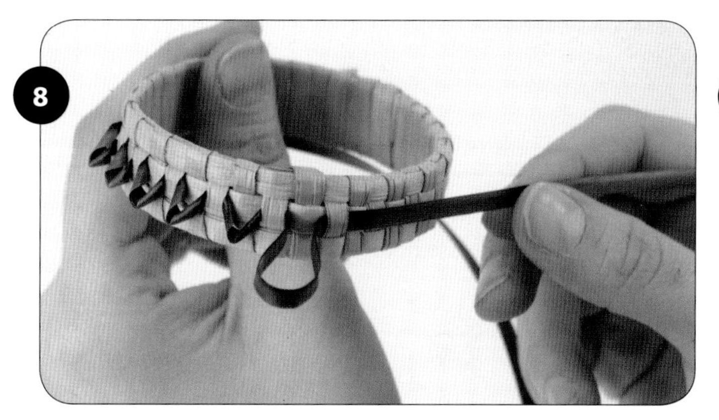

**8.** Insert the weaving strand through the adjacent loop with the cuticle side up.

**9.** Before pulling the weaving strand tight, grasp the top of the loop and twist the loop so that the cuticle side is now down.

A second variation involves twisting the curl in the opposite direction for each curl to evoke a zig zag effect.

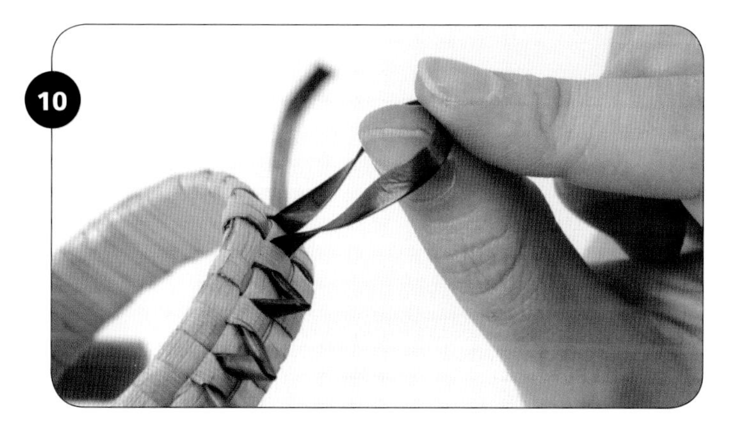

**10.** Another view showing twisting the loop so that the cuticle side is down. Now slowly pull the weaving strand taut so that two curls form. Notice that the cuticle side shows on the curl.

# *Project 14:* Criss-Cross Embellishment

**WHAT YOU'LL NEED:**

- 3/4-inch wide Three-Warp Strand Checkerboard Bracelet (page 21), with 1/4-inch warps
- 1/4-inch *koana*, dyed

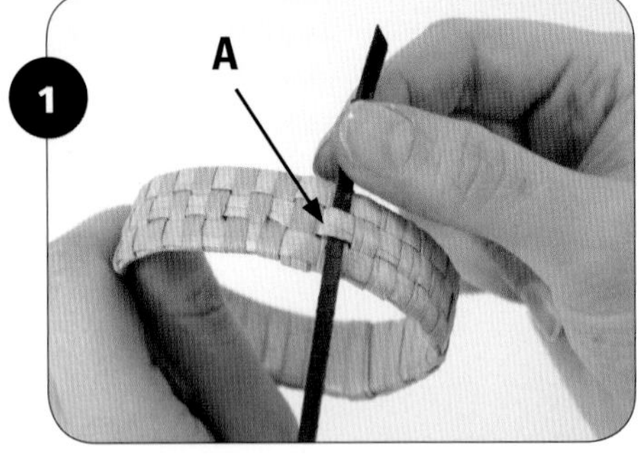


**1.** Insert the weaver, cuticle side down, under a loop of the middle warp strand (A).

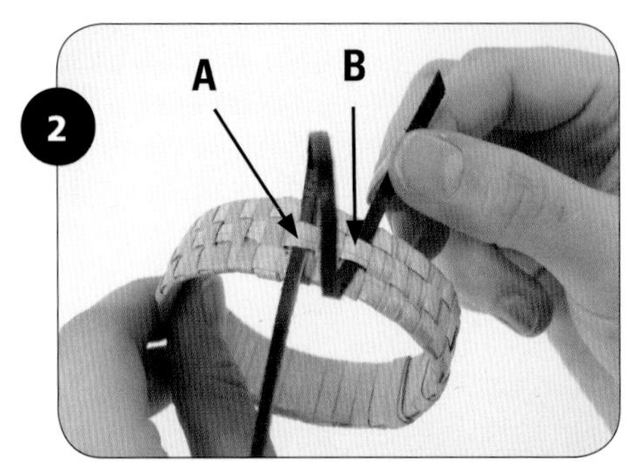


**2.** Bring the *koana* back around the middle warp and insert, cuticle side down under the adjacent loop (B) of the middle warp strand.

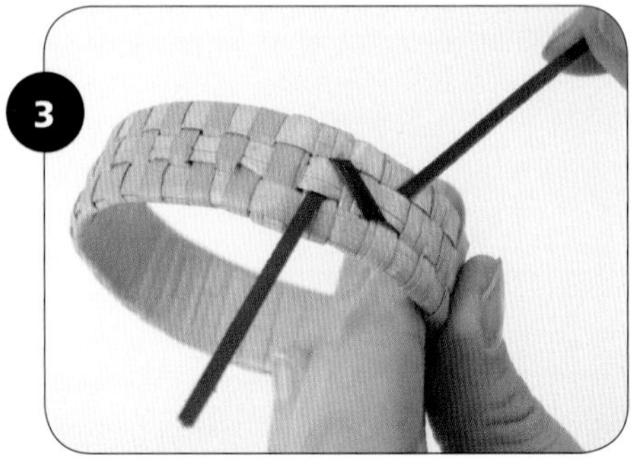


**3.** Pull the loop of the *koana* taut. The cuticle side of the loop should be up and showing.

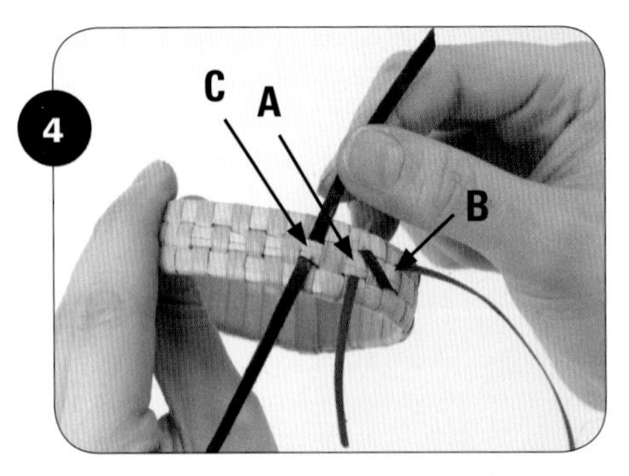


**4.** Bring the *koana* to the left and insert, cuticle side down, in the same direction as the previous two insertions, under the loop (C) to the left of the beginning insertion (A).

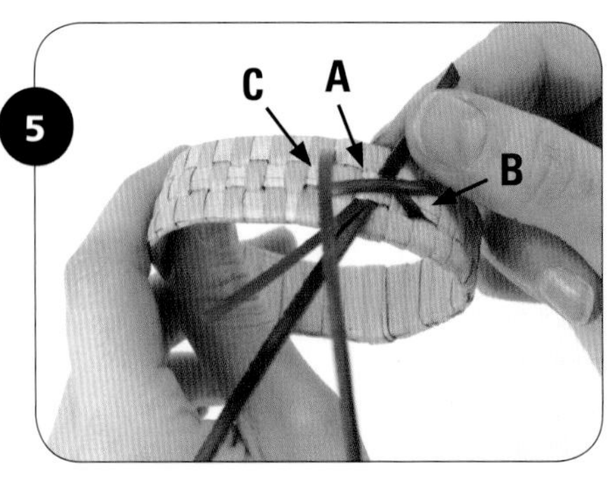


**5.** Bring the *koana* from (C) and insert under the first loop (A).

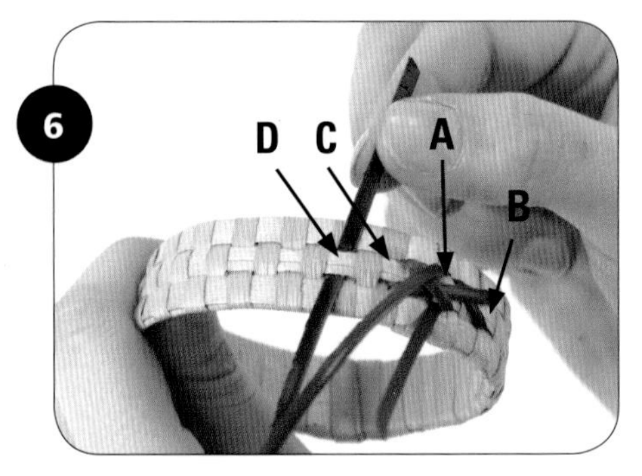


**6.** Pull the loop tight and bring the *koana* to left and insert under the loop (D) to the left of loop (C).

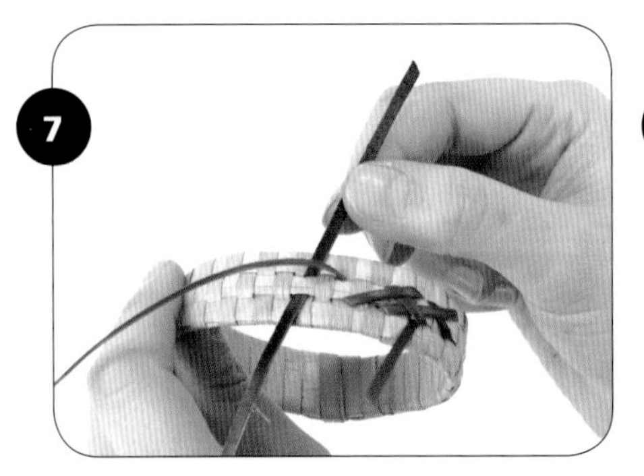


**7.** Continue with this pattern all the way around the bracelet.

**8.** The finished bracelet.

# *Project 15:*
# KUUIPO Domed Bracelet
## Using the alphabet grid

**PREPARATION:**

Consult the alphabet grid in the Appendix. Use a sheet of graph paper and block out a space that is 11 squares by 60 to 80 squares. A bracelet woven with 1/8-inch weavers will need an average of 60 to 80 squares, depending on the outer diameter of the band. A bracelet of 2-1/3 inches in diameter will have approximately 60 wraps of *koana.* A bracelet 3-1/4 inches in diameter will have approximately 80 wraps.

Leave the top two rows of squares blank as well as the bottom 2 rows. Your plaited word will fit in the seven rows of squares in the middle of the blocked out area.

Transfer the letters, one by one, to your sheet of graph paper. Fill in the squares with a pencil or pen. Work slowly and carefully. Leave one column blank between each letter.

The word we'll use in this project is "kuuipo", which in Hawaiian means "such a sweetheart." It is a word often found on vintage Hawaiian gold jewelry, including bracelets and pendants. It seems appropriate for a gift for a true friend or relative. You could also use your name, your Hawaiian name, "mom," "dad," "grandma," "grandpa," or any word or phrase which comes to mind. For our project we'll use "kuuipo" so that you can practice how to weave the letters into the bracelet.

**BRACELET PATTERN:**

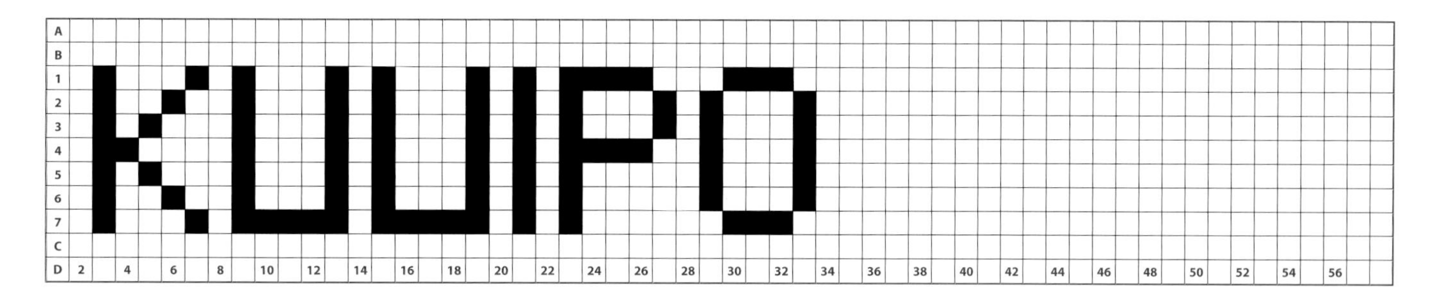


For this pattern to read well you will need a minimum of eleven warp strands which includes seven warps for the letters and two blank rows above and below the word.

The bracelet project will use warp and weft strands stripped to 1/8-inch wide.

The bracelet will be woven in the same way as Project 8 with the dark strands being the warp and the light strands the weft strand.

Prepare the band with an extra length of *lauhala* to make the band thicker. Attach the 16-inch length of stripped dark *lauhala* taped in place. We will need a minimum of 35 wraps with the weaving strand. If our bracelet is 3-1/4 inches in diameter, it will have a circumference of $3.25\varpi$ or 10.21 inches. If you divide 10.21 by .125 (1/8-inch) the result is 81.68 or 81 wraps around a 3-1/4 inch diameter bracelet—enough for 80 characters.

We could weave "kuuipo" twice with 10 spaces between each word (30 spaces allowed for the word plus an extra 10 blank spaces x 2 equals 80 characters.)

Strip a length of *lauhala* into a 1-3/8-inch width bracelet coil. As you've learned in Project 8, instead of stripping the last 14 inches of the band, strip a 16-inch length of dyed *lauhala* into 1/8-inch *koana*, leaving the first 2 inches still connected and taped it to the bracelet coil.

**1.** Hold the wrist band with the eleven dyed warp strands facing to the right. The weaving *koana* are also 1/8-inch wide.

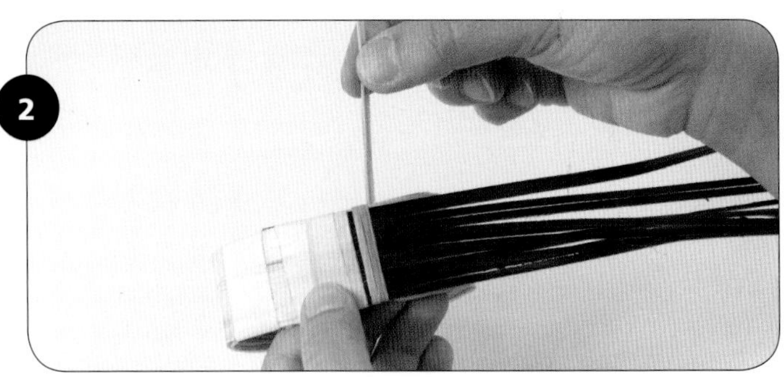


**2.** Row 1 and 2: Wrap over all warp strands twice.

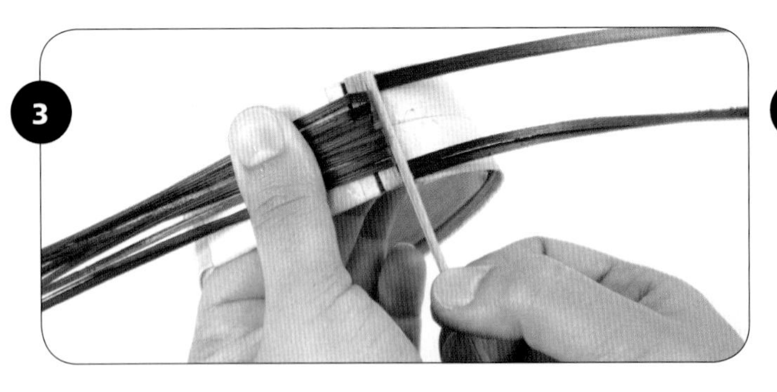


**3.** Row 3: Fold back strands 1, 2, 3, 4, 5, 6 and 7. Wrap over warp strands A and B, under warp strands 1, 2, 3, 4, 5, 6 and 7, and over warp strands C and D.

**4.** Row 4: Fold back strand 4. Wrap over warp strands A, B, 1, 2, 3, under warp strand 4, and over 5, 6, 7, C, and D.

**5.** Row 5: Fold back strands 3 and 5. Wrap over warp strands A, B, 1 and 2, under warp strand 3, over warp strand 4, under warp strand 5, and over 6, 7, C and D.

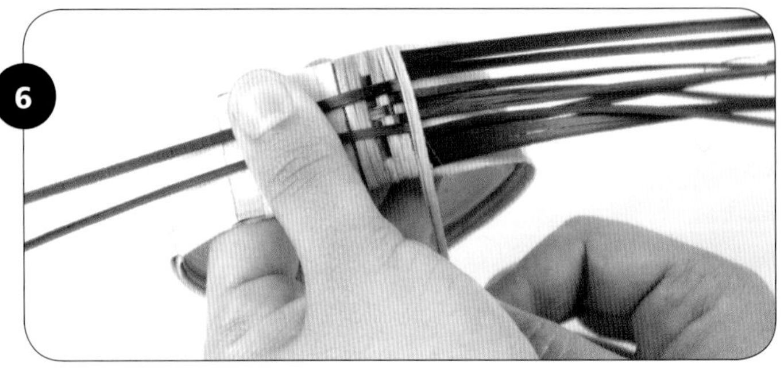


**6.** Row 6: Fold back strands 2 and 6. Wrap over A, B, 1, under 2, over 3, 4, 5, under 6, over 7, C and D.

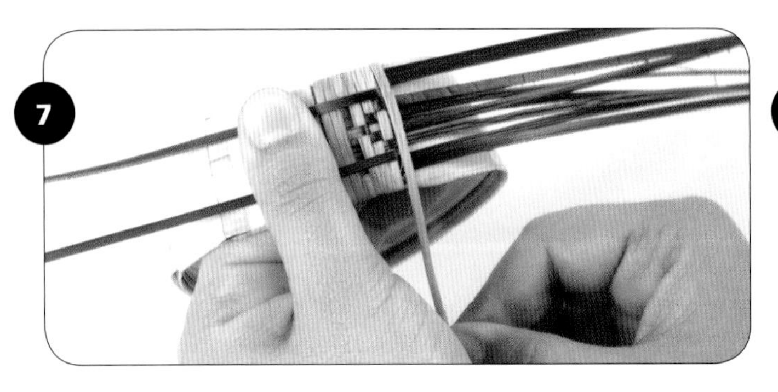


**7.** Row 7: Fold back strands 1 and 7. Wrap over A and B, under 1, over 2, 3, 4, 5, 6, under 7, over C and D.

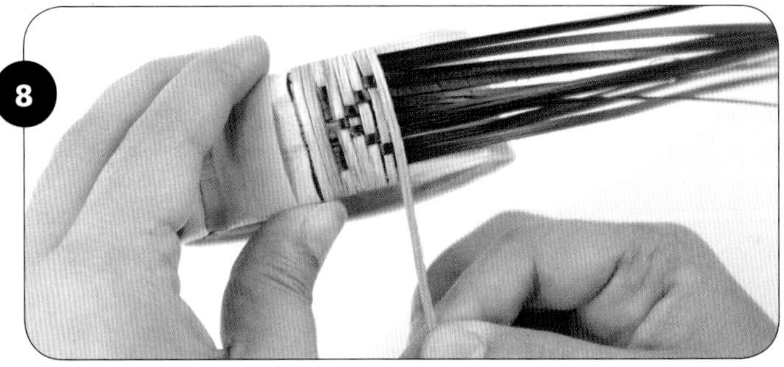


**8.** Row 8: Wrap over all warp strands.

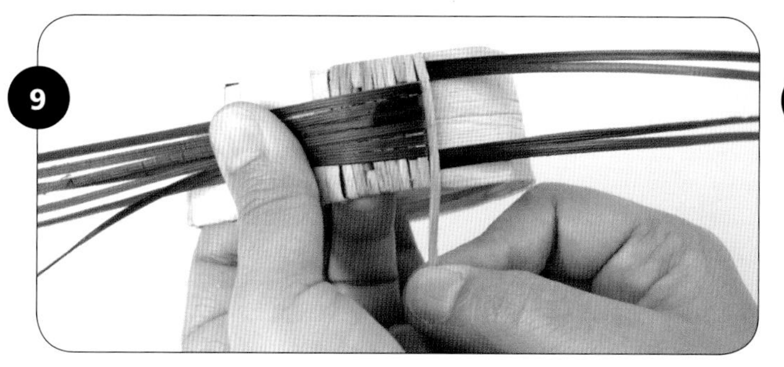

**9.** Row 9: Fold back strands 1, 2, 3, 4, 5, 6 and 7. Wrap over A and B, under 1, 2, 3, 4, 5, 6 and 7, over C and D.

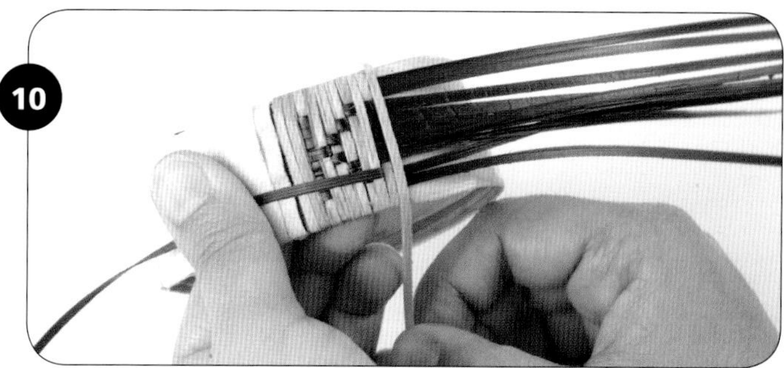

**10.** Row 10: Fold back strand 7. Wrap over A, B, 1, 2, 3, 4, 5 and 6, under 7, over C and D.

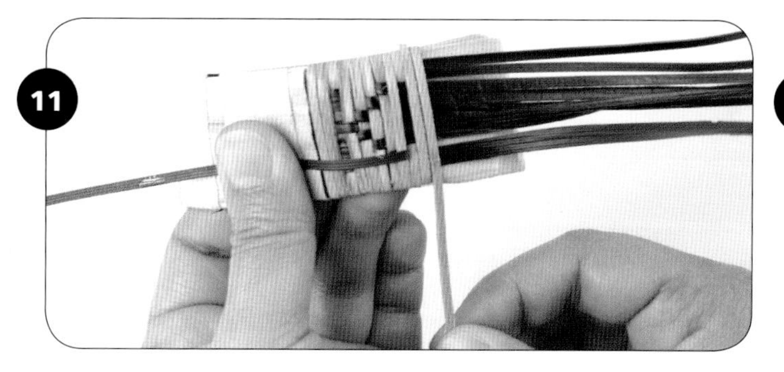

**11.** Row 11: Fold back strand 7. Wrap over A, B, 1, 2, 3, 4, 5 and 6, under 7, over C and D.

**12:** Row 12: Fold back strand 7. Wrap over A, B, 1, 2, 3, 4, 5 and 6, under 7, over C and D.

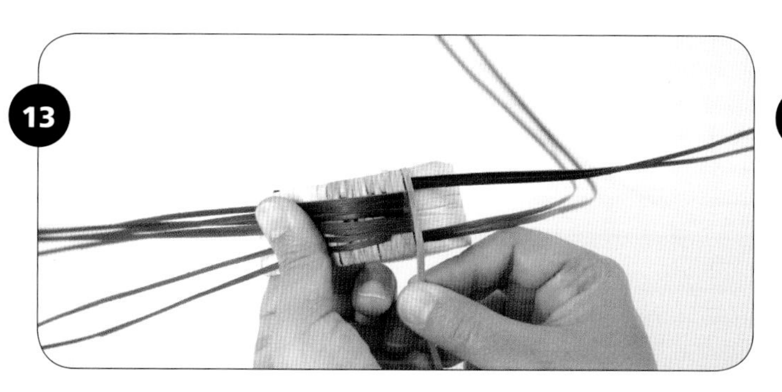

**13.** Row 13 : Fold back strands 1, 2, 3, 4, 5, 6 and 7. Wrap over A, B, under 1, 2, 3, 4, 5 and 6 and 7, over C and D.

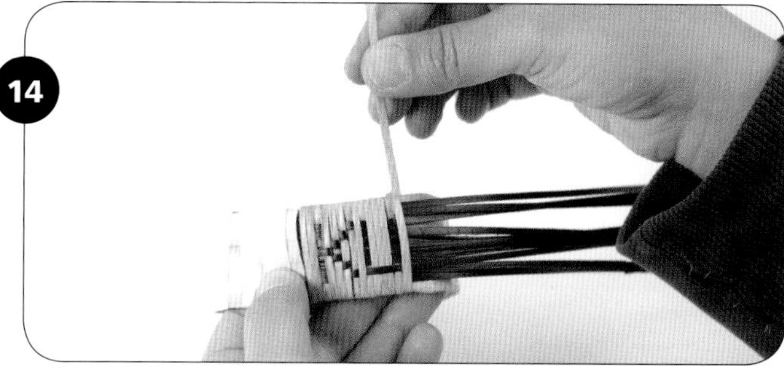

**14.** Row 14: Wrap over all warp strands.

**15.** Row 15: Fold back strands 1, 2, 3, 4, 5, 6 and 7. Wrap over A and B, under 1, 2, 3, 4, 5, 6 and 7, over C and D.

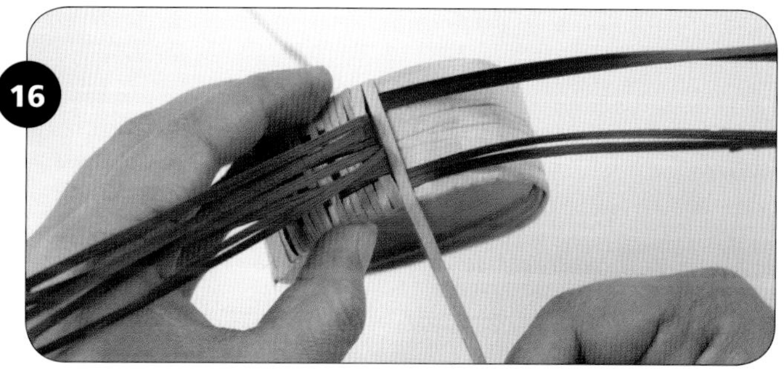

**16.** Row 16: Over A, B, 1, 2, 3, 4, 5 and 6, under 7, over C and D.

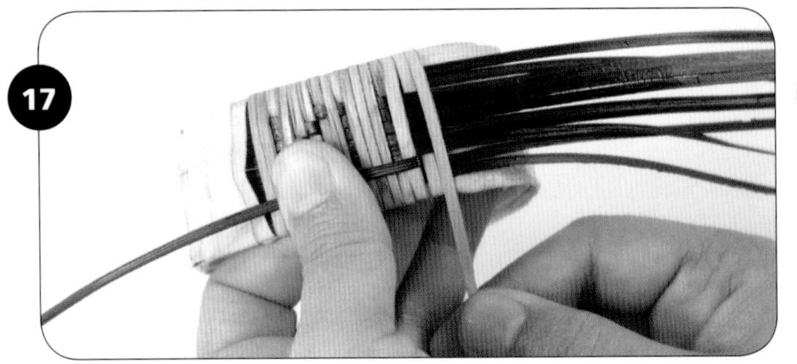


**17.** Row 17: Over A, B, 1, 2, 3, 4, 5 and 6, under 7, over C and D.

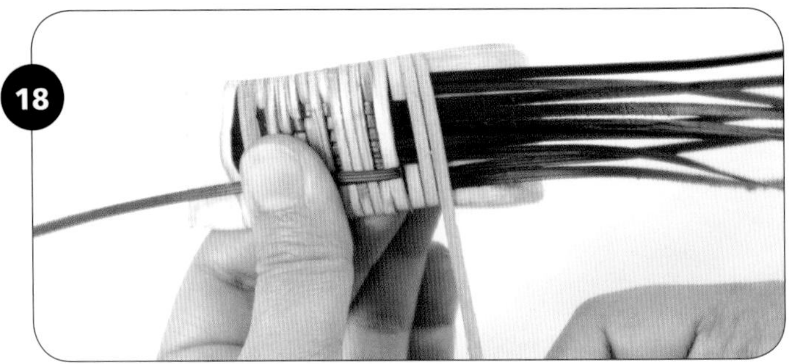


**18.** Row 18: Over A, B, 1, 2, 3, 4, 5 and 6, under 7, over C and D.

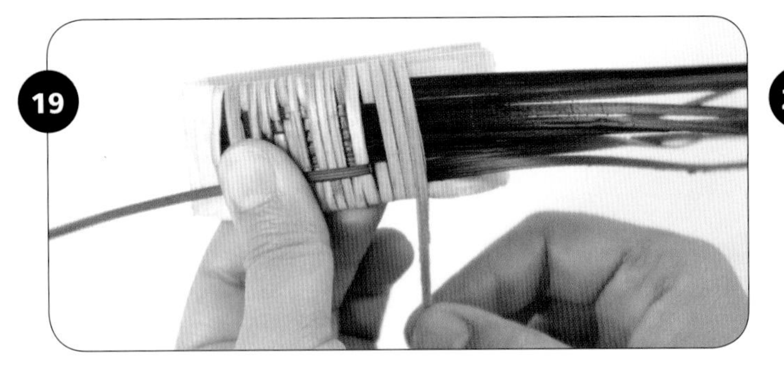


**19.** Row 19: Over A, B, 1, 2, 3, 4, 5 and 6, under 7, over C and D.

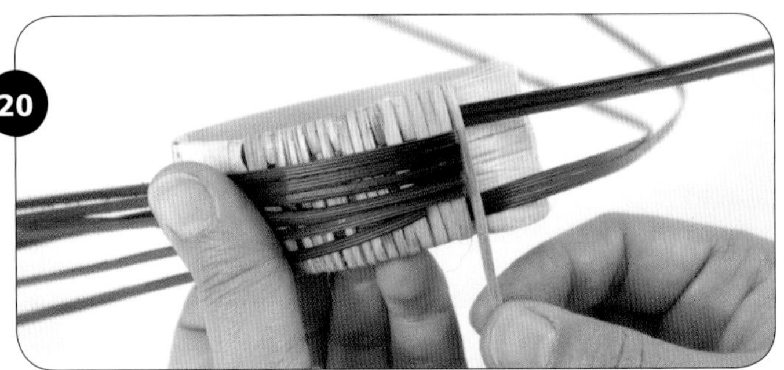


**20.** Row 20: Over A, B, under 1, 2, 3, 4, 5, 6, and 7, over C and D.

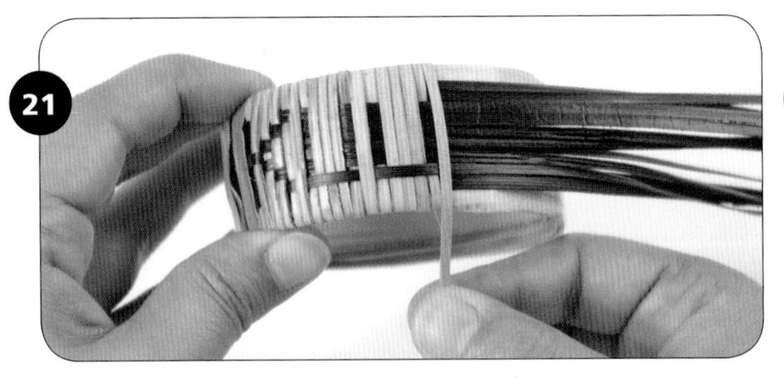


**21.** Row 21: Wrap over all warp strands.

**22.** Row 22: Over A and B, under 1, 2, 3, 4, 5, 6 and 7, over C and D.

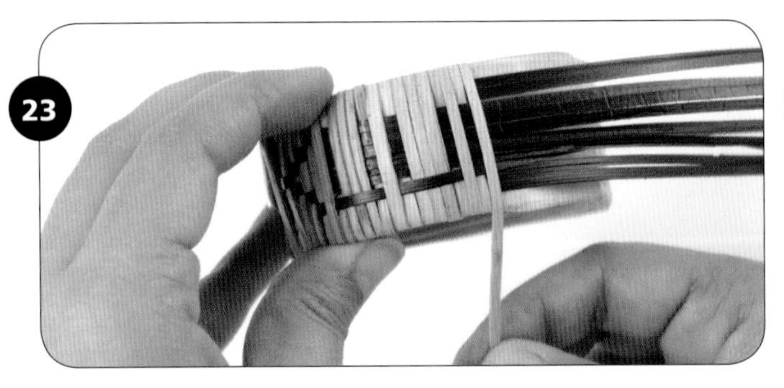


**23.** Row 23: Wrap over all warp strands.

**24.** Row 24: Over A and B, under 1, 2, 3, 4, 5, 6 and 7, over C and D.

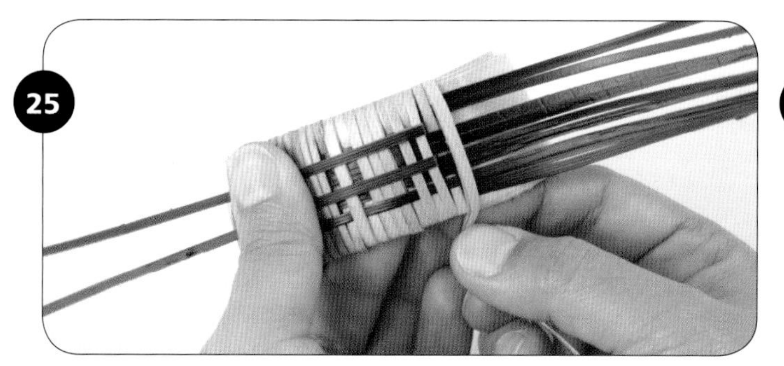


**25.** Row 25: Over A and B, under 1, over 2 and 3, under 4, over 5, 6, 7, C and D.

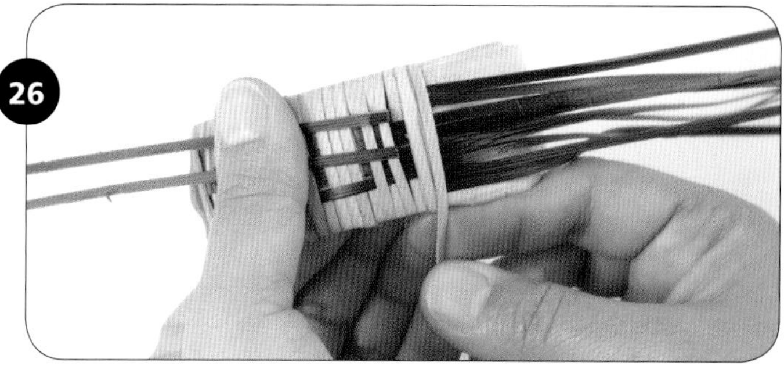


**26.** Row 26: Over A and B, under 1, over 2 and 3, under 4, over 5, 6, 7, C and D.

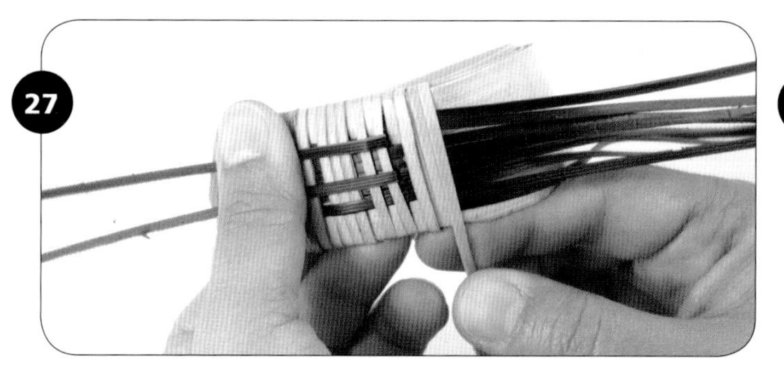


**27.** Row 27: Over A and B, under 1, over 2 and 3, under 4, over 5, 6, 7, C and D.

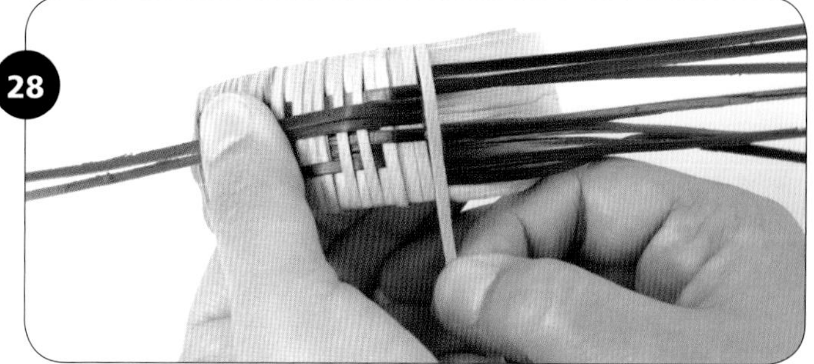


**28.** Row 28: Over A, B and 1, under 2 and 3, over 4, 5, 6, 7, C and D.

**29.** Row 29: Wrap over all warp strands.

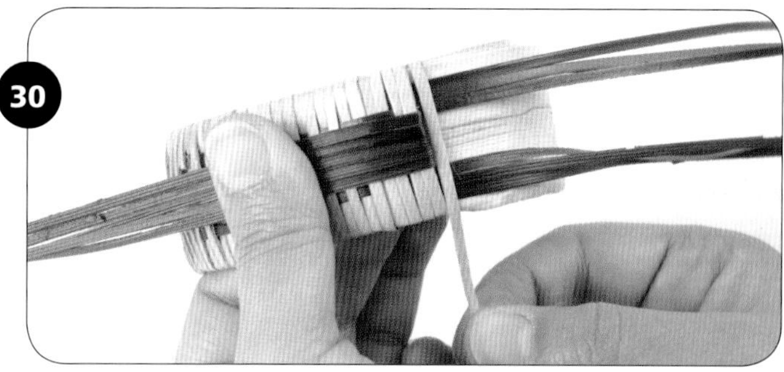


**30.** Row 30: Over A, B and 1, under 2, 3, 4, 5 and 6, over 7, C and D.

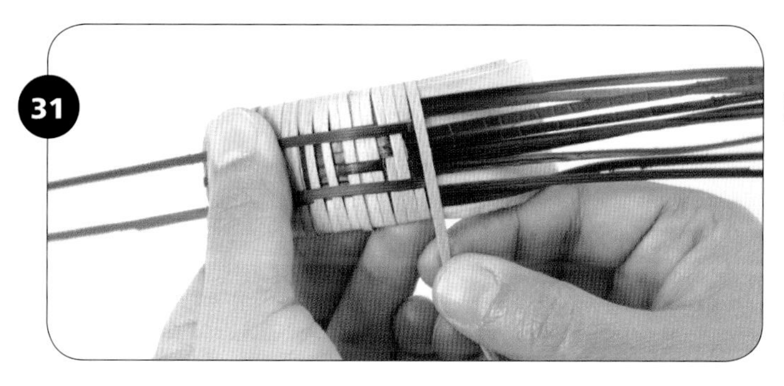


**31.** Row 31: Over A and B, under 1, over 2, 3, 4, 5 and 6, under 7, over C and D.

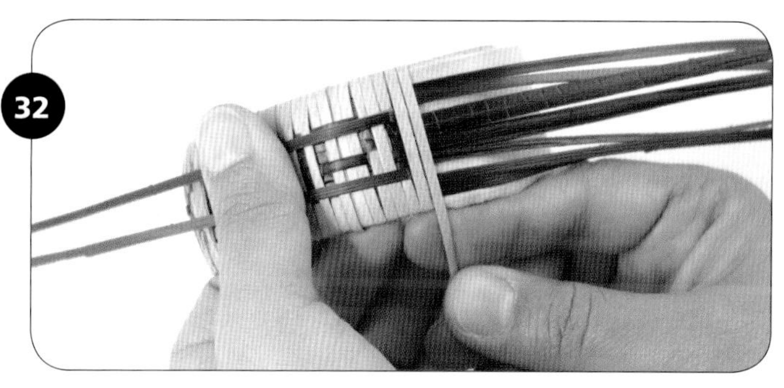


**32.** Row 32: Over A and B, under 1, over 2, 3, 4, 5 and 6, under 7, over C and D.

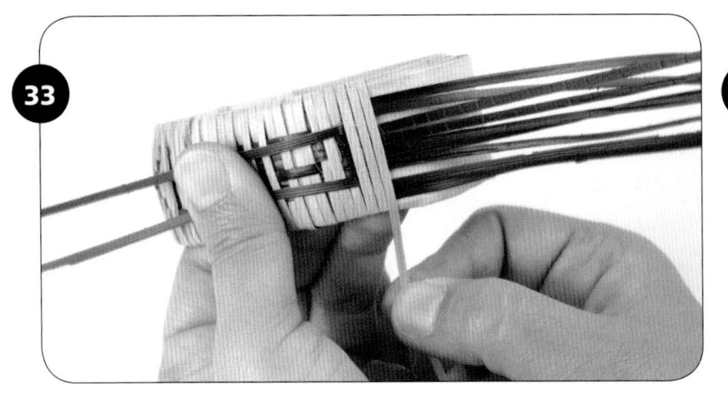

**33.** Row 33: Over A and B, under 1, over 2, 3, 4, 5 and 6, under 7, over C and D.

**34.** Row 34: Over A, B and 1, under 2 and 3, over 4, 5, 6, 7, C and D.

**35:** Row 35 and 36: Wrap over all warp strands.

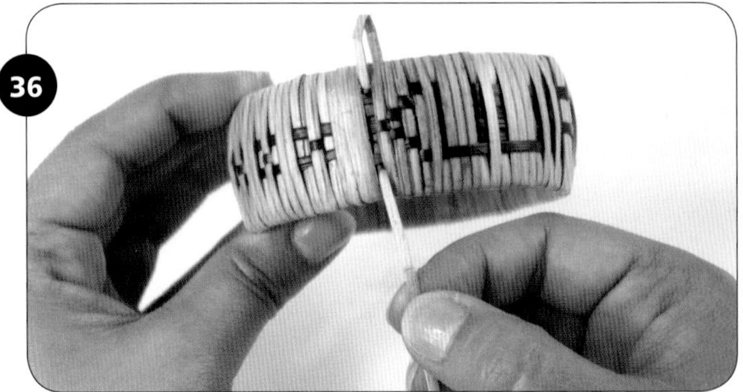

**36.** Finish the bracelet by bringing the last wrap through a letter where it will be under at least two warp strands, to secure it.

**37.** Trim the strand flush with the lower warp strand.

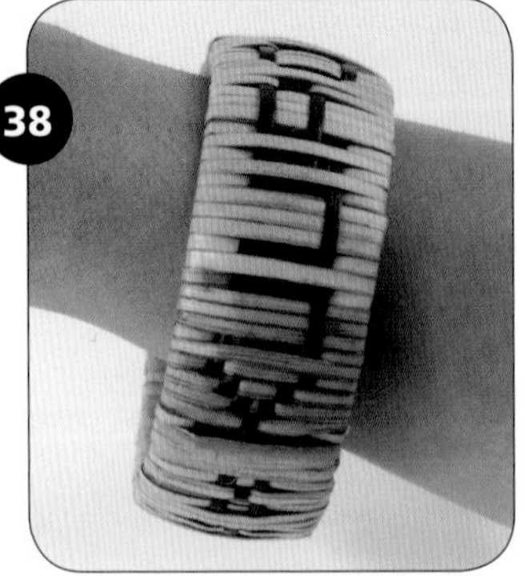

**38.** The finished bracelet.

**39.** If you are less than, or exactly halfway around your band, you can weave "kuuipo" a second time, or another word.

# *Project 16:* Lauhala Hairband

**WHAT YOU'LL NEED:**
- inexpensive plastic hairband (available in fabric and crafts stores)
- scissors
- masking tape
- *lauhala*

**1.** Cover the top and bottom of the hairband with the center section of a length of *lauhala*. Wrap the leaf around the ends of the hairband and secure with masking tape. Use a pair of scissors to trim away and *lauhala* that might be wider than the hairband.

**2.** With the widest portion of this particular hairband (1-1/4 inch) we needed ten *koana*, 1/8-inch wide. They are taped to the middle of the hairband, making sure that the overall length of the warp *koana* is longer than the length of the hairband.

**3.** Begin weaving in the middle of the hairband in a simple over under checkerboard. The beginning of the weft strand is left hanging.

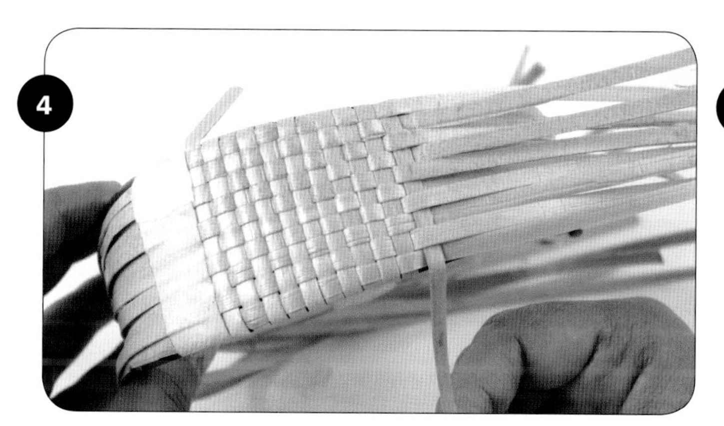

**4.** As the weaving progresses notice that the hairband is becoming narrower.

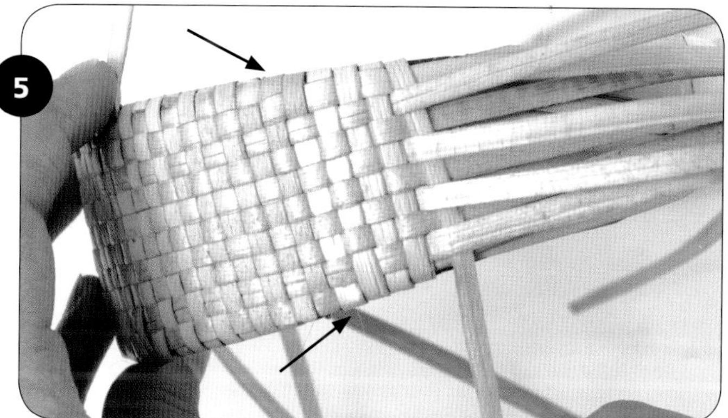

**5.** As the hairband frame narrows, drop the two outer warp strands from the weaving pattern by simply ignoring and wrapping over them.

**6.** We drop two more outer warp strands from the weaving pattern.

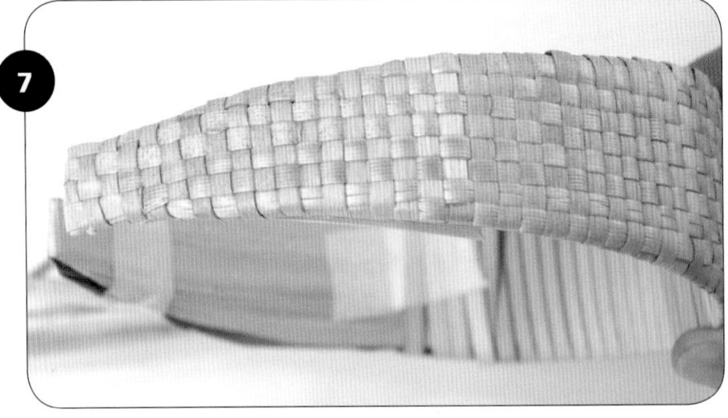

**7.** Detail of the end of the hairband showing how the narrowing from ten warp strands to four warp strands was achieved without disrupting the flow of the checkerboard weaving.

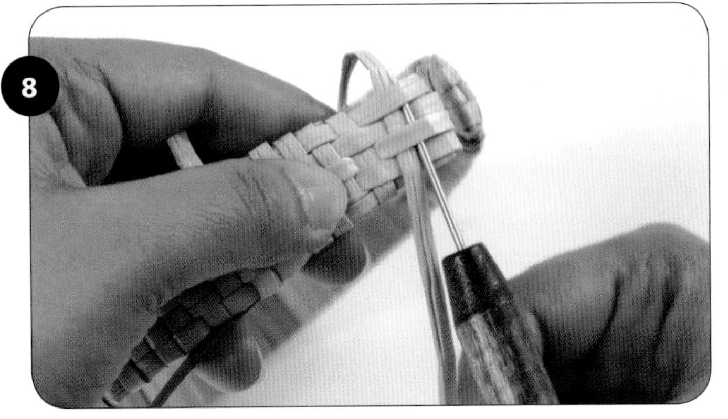

**8.** When there is only room for 5 more rows, bend the last four warp strands around the end of the hairband. Use the awl to help make a space in the weave to slip the wrapping strand.

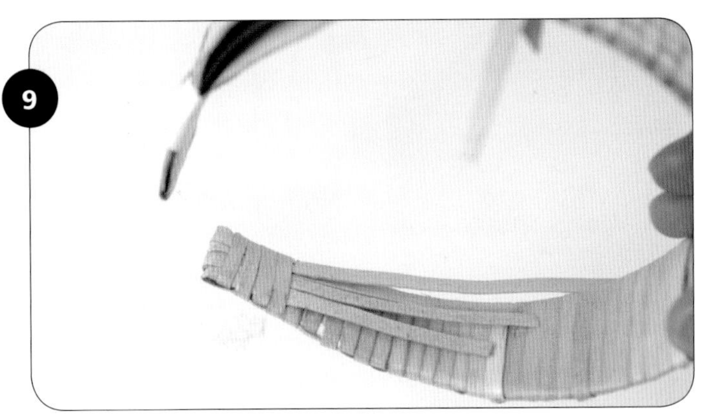

**9.** The last 4 or 5 rows cover the ends of the warp strands. The weave anchors the end of the wrapping strand.

**10.** When the weft is pulled taut, trim the ends of the warp strands flush.

**11.** Completed *lauhala* hairband.

**12.** Variation: hairband with the addition of a couple of *lauhala* roses.

# *Project 17:* Lauhala Cords

Our Polynesian ancestors, being sailors, had many uses for ropes, lines and string, and the main sources they had for making ropes and string were the leaves of the pandanus (*hala*) plant, the inner bark from hibiscus (*hau*) plants and the husks of the coconut (*nie*) tree. Cordage is made by twisting two fibers together. Rope is made by twisting lengths of cordage together. Cordage made from the coconut husks, was used for weaving fishing nets and lines that would be in seawater for lengths of time. The pandanus sails were sewn together with lines made from *lauhala* and *hau* fiber. *Hau* fibers were also used to make the strong lines for controlling the sails and for stowing gear.

The following project is to introduce you to the joy of turning a leaf into a length of strong string. This is a skill that might come to be very useful someday when you need to tie something together and there just isn't a piece of string handy.

In the meantime, you'll learn to make a wonderful friendship bracelet or anklet that your friend will be proud to wear for many weeks.

**WHAT YOU'LL NEED:**

- one *koana*, 1/2-inch wide and about 36 inches long

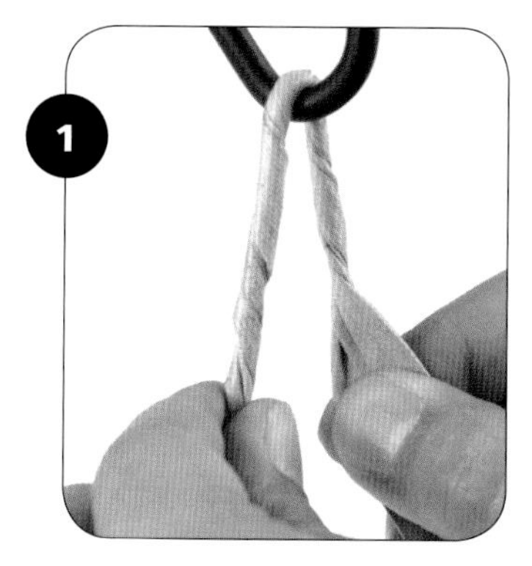

**1.** Twist the middle of the *koana* so that it forms a rope-like appearance. Hang the *koana* on a hook or have a friend hold the middle of the strand. Twist both halves of the strand from left to right.

**2.** Take the strand that was on the right and cross it in front of the strand that was on the left. Change hands. Continue to twist each half from left to right.

**3.** As you twist the individual strands from left to right, continue to cross the right strand in front of the left strand and change hands.

**4.** Your twisted *lauhala* should look like the photo. Try to make your twists uniform and neat.

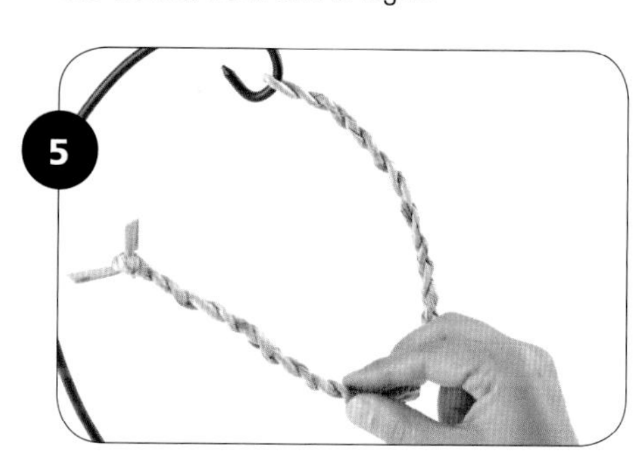

**5.** When you get to the end of the strands, tie them together into a thick knot.

**6.** Slip the loop at the beginning of the twist off of the hook. Open the loop a little wider by slightly untwisting and insert the knot from the other end through the loop. Let the twist close.

**7.** This is an example of a shorter twisted *lauhala* strand.

# *Project 18:* Lauhala Rose

There are two methods of weaving a rose from ribbons or leaves. I illustrated one of the methods in *How to Weave Hawaiian Coconut Palm Fronds*. The following method is found throughout Polynesia, along the shores of the Indian Ocean, as well as in New Zealand. The construction is purely through folding rather than twisting.

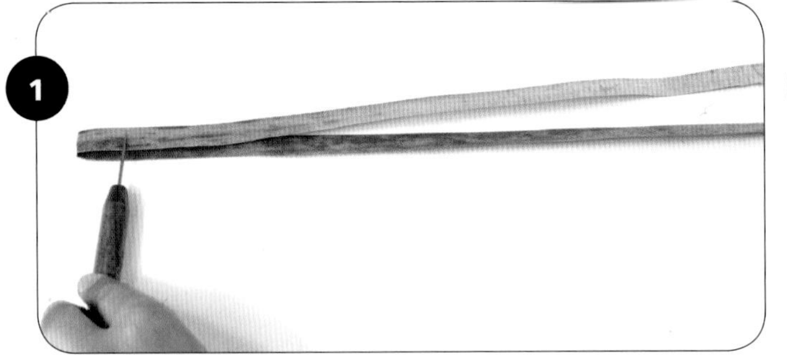

**1.** Strip one *lauhala* into a 1/2-inch wide *koana*. Fold it in half with the "good" sides together.

**2.** Rotate the fold so the two halves are at right angles to each other.

**3.** Take the lower strand and fold it so that if faces up.

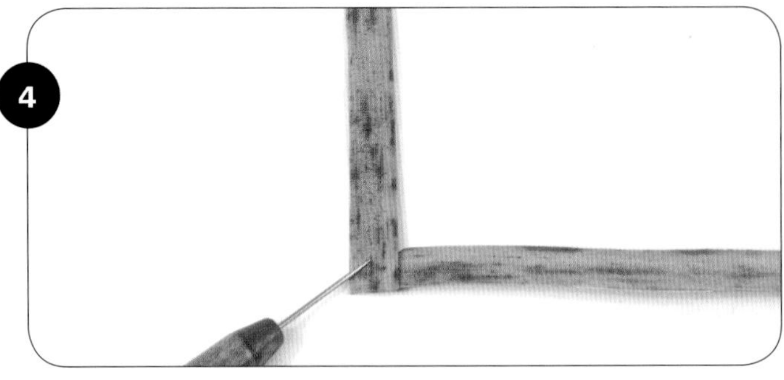

**4.** Here is the completed fold. Keep the crease in line with the strand pointing to the right.

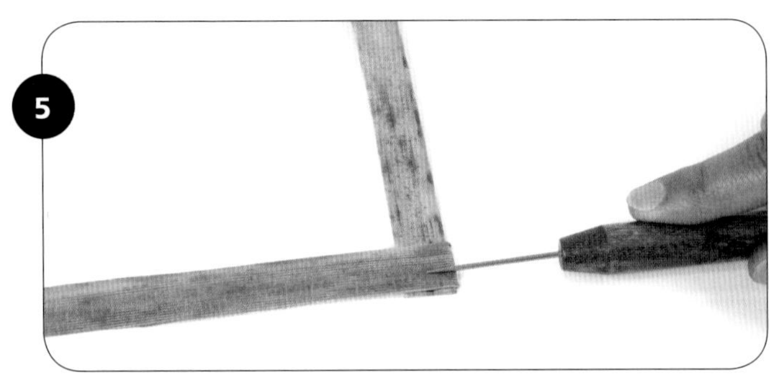

**5.** Take the strand pointing to the right and fold it so that it now faces to the left. Keep the crease in line with the upper strand.

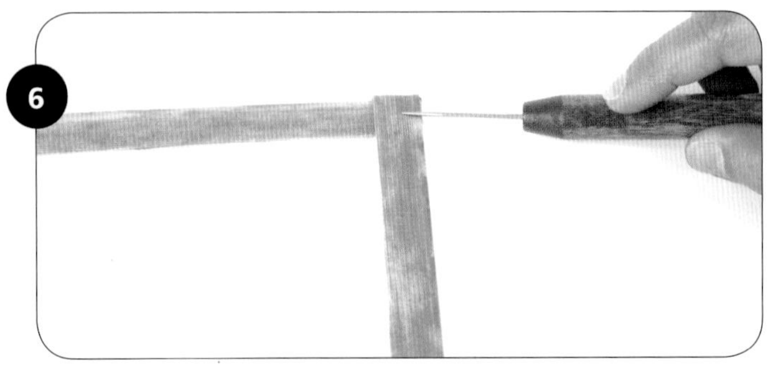

**6.** Take the upper strand and fold it so that it faces down. Keep the creases on top of each other.

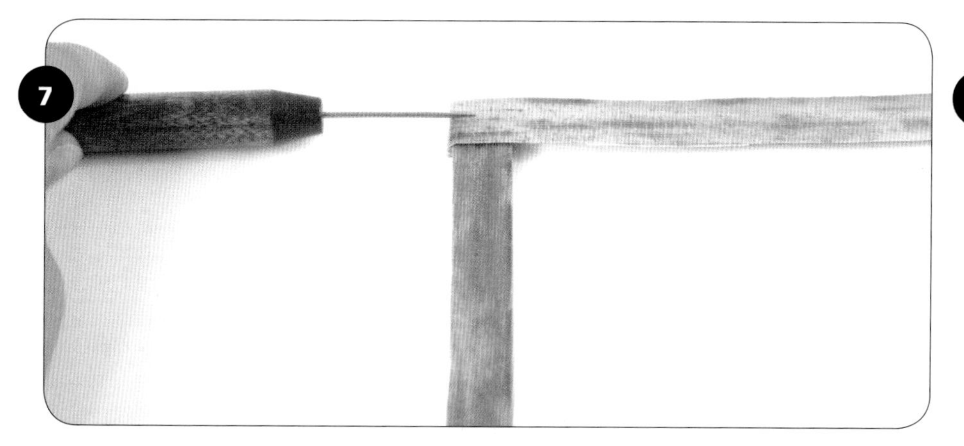

**7.** Take the strand pointing to the left and fold it so that it faces to the right.

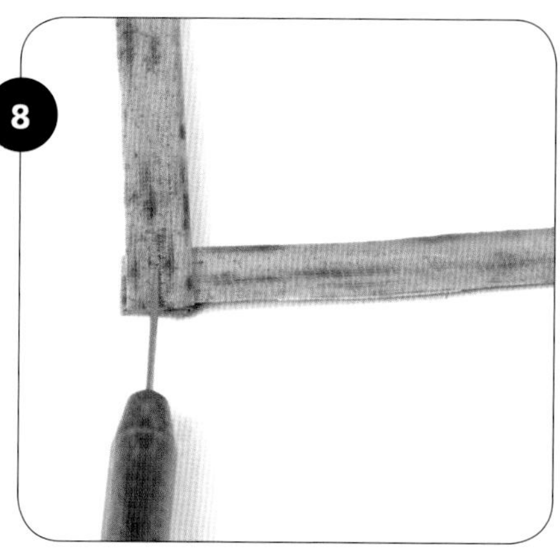

**8.** Take the strand pointing down and fold it so that it is pointing up.

**9.** If you relax the folded corner, this is what it should look like.

**10.** Continue folding so that you fold in all four directions for three complete cycles.

**11.** Hold the two ends so that the right hand is holding the "center" leaf and the left hand is holding the outer leaf.

**12.** With the right hand, pull on the center leaf to slowly begin to collapse the folded tower.

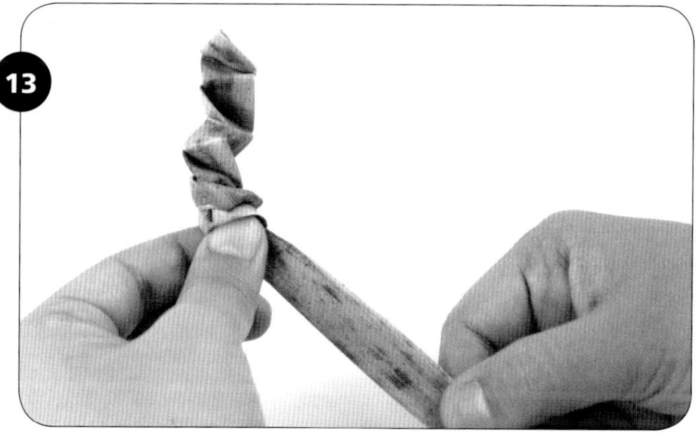

**13.** Continuing to pull with the right hand.

**14.** The tower has almost completely collapsed but there is a little more to go.

**15.** The collapsed tower has now formed the rose.

**16.** A detail of the center of the rose.

**17.** Tie the two leaves together to keep the rose from unraveling.

**18.** The completed rose with a bow.

**19.** The completed rose woven into the bracelet from Project 5.

# *Project 19:* Lauhala Ball

The *lauhala* ball can be found throughout Hawai'i and Polynesia. In some cultures a fresh *hala* leaf is used to cook small portions of rice. The ball is filled with uncooked rice and dropped into boiling water to cook an individual portion. The green *hala* leaf imparts a fragrance to the rice as a seasoning.

**WHAT YOU'LL NEED:**

- two *lauhala* stripped to 1/2-inch wide and 24- to 36-inches long *koana*, soaked and prepared
- red, green, yellow and blue permanent markers

We have colored both halves of two *koana* so that you can follow each strand as it interweaves and easily locate the correct strand to overweave as you finish this project. After making two or three balls, you'll have the weaving technique mastered and there will be no further need to color the strands. Your friends will think it's magic!

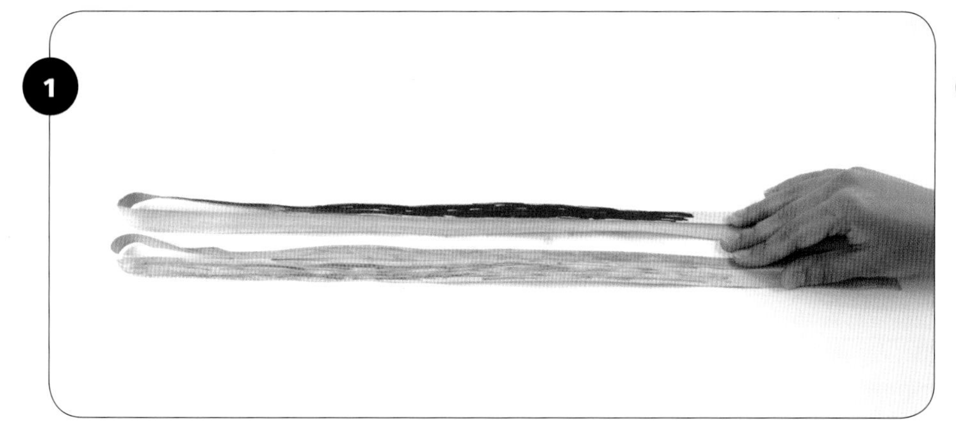

**1.** Find the halfway point for each *koana*. Color each half of the *koana*, only on the good side. One strip will be red and green. The second strip will be yellow and blue.

**2.** Fold each strip in half. Make sure both good sides are visible. Interweave the two strips as pictured in the photograph.

**3.** Bring the two folds together as tight as possible but still keeping each strand flat. Take your time and carefully work the strands together.

**4.** Bring the yellow strand under the blue strand and parallel to the red and green strands.

**5.** Weave the green strand over the red strand, under the yellow strand and parallel to the blue strand. Allow the beginning of the braid to curl away from you.

**6.** Bring the blue strand under the green strand, parallel to the yellow and red strands.

**7.** Interweave the red strand over the yellow strand and under the blue strand, keeping it parallel to the green strand.

**8.** Pull the strands taut and allow the beginning of the plait to continue to curl away from. Weave the green strand under the red strand.

**9.** Weave the yellow strand over the blue strand and under the green strand.

**10.** Weave the red strand under the yellow strand.

**11.** Weave the blue strand over the green strand and under the red strand.

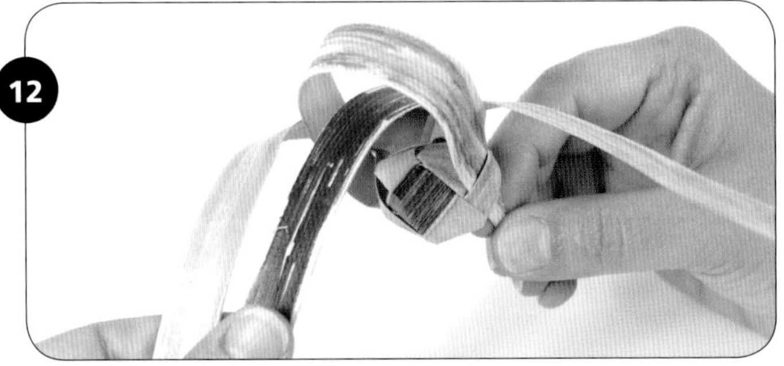

**12.** Pick up the red strand and study the pattern on the ball. There should be a red strand woven into the ball immediately below, or very close.

**13.** Insert the red strand under the woven green strand. This should lock all of the strands in place.

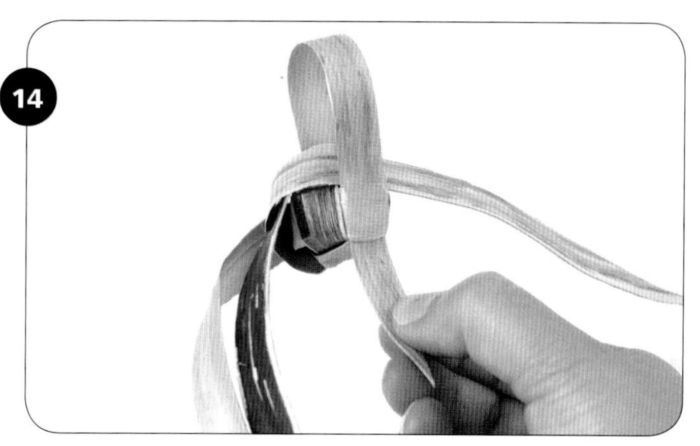


**14.** Insert the green strand under the woven yellow strand and along with the already woven green strand.

**15.** Insert the yellow strand under the blue strand and along with the already woven yellow strand.

**16.** Insert the blue strand under the green strand and along with the already woven blue strand.

**17.** Insert the green strand under the red strand and along the already woven green strand.

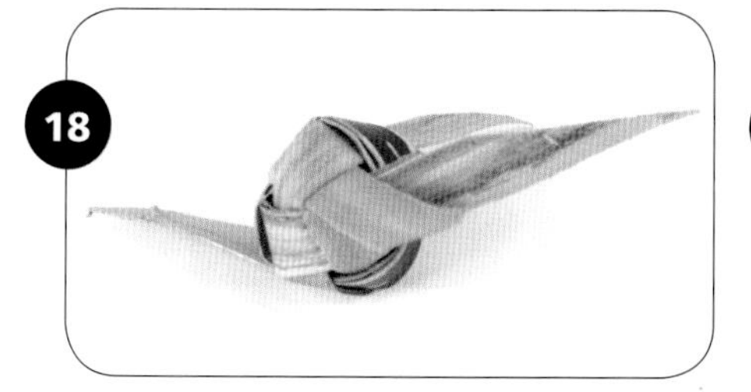


**18.** Pull all of the strands tight. Continue interweaving all of the strands until the ends are too short to interweave any more.

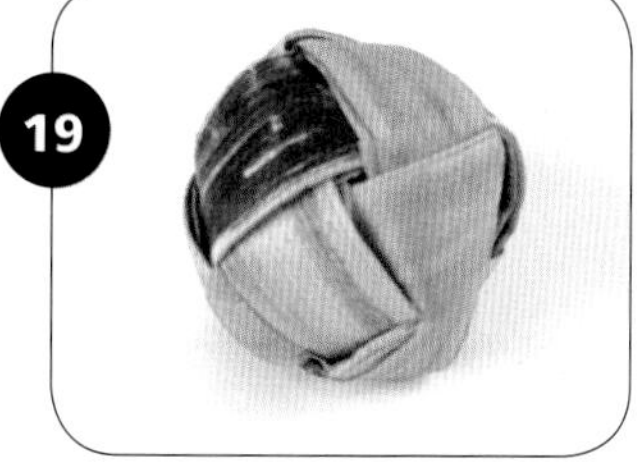


**19.** Trim the ends so that they pull back inside the weave and are hidden.

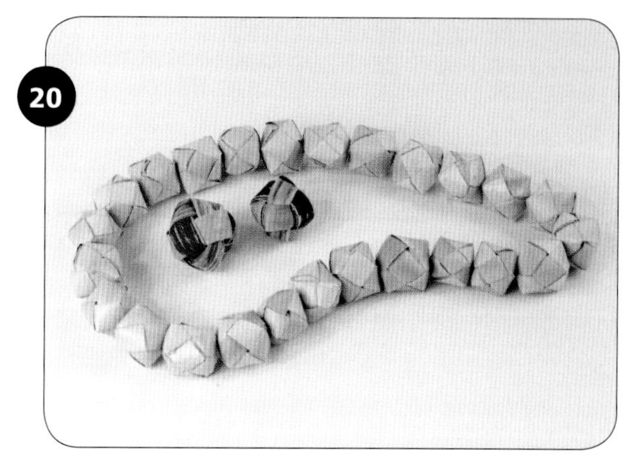


**20.** A lei of *lauhala* balls.

A B C D E F G H
I J K L M N O P Q
R S T U V W X
Y Z

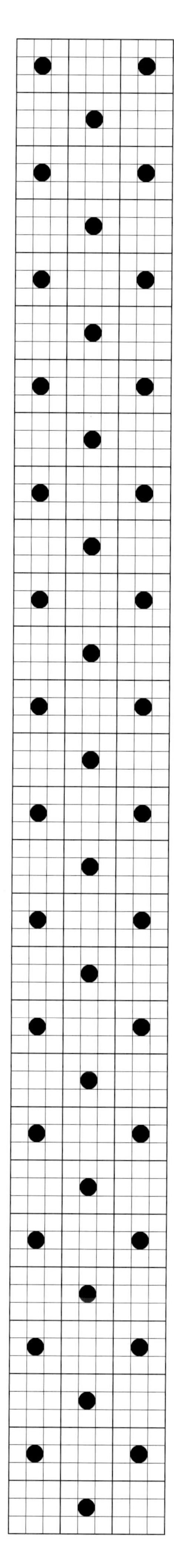

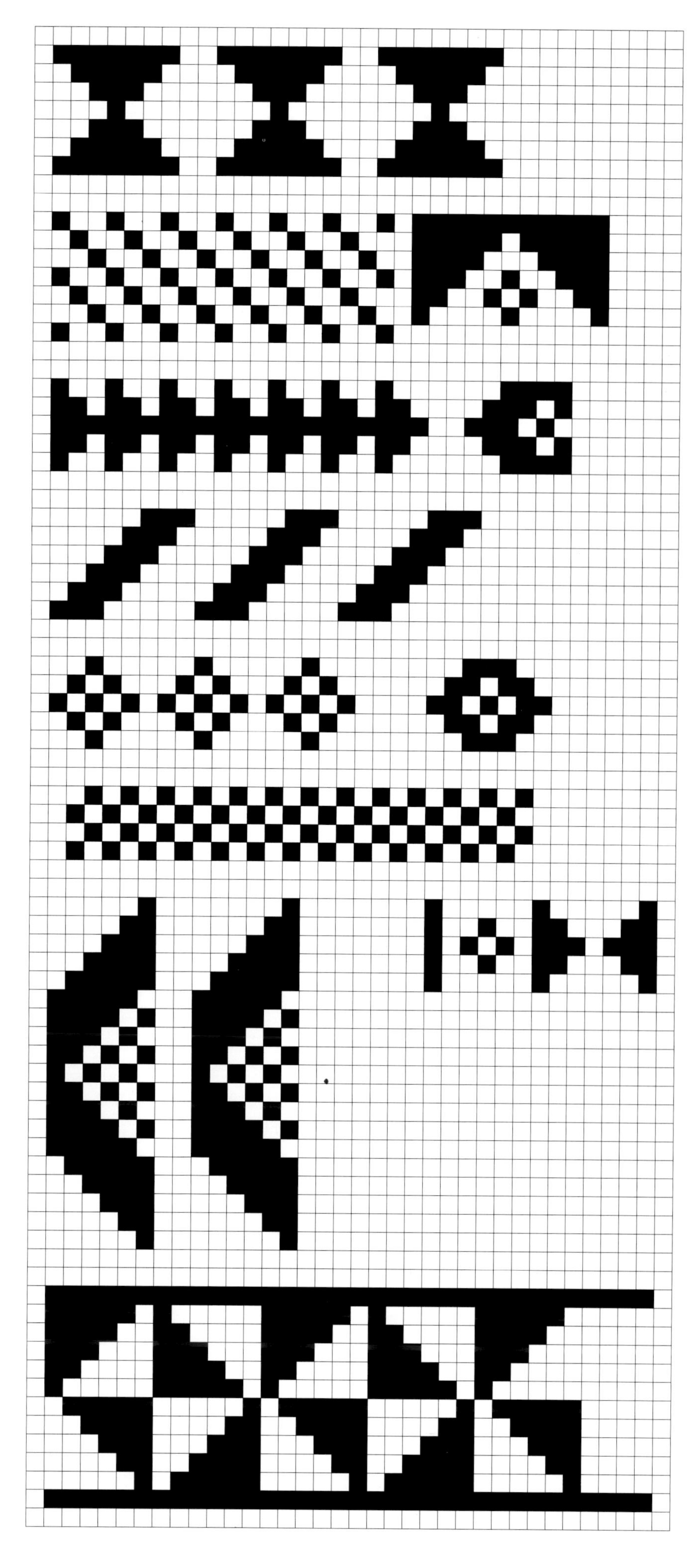

# Appendix

## Hawaiian Terms:

| | |
|---|---|
| **hala hinano** | male pandanus tree, which bears the very fragrant hinano blossom |
| **hala hua** | fruit-bearing female pandanus tree |
| **huehuelo** | tip or tail of a leaf |
| **ki** | bundle of 40 hala leaves |
| **koana** | prepared *lauhala* strips (cut to size) |
| **ku** | warp strands |
| **kuka'a** | roll of *lauhala* |
| **lauhala** | leaf of pandanus, or hala, tree |
| **lei** | garland of flowers, shells, leaves, feathers, pods, nuts, strung together and worn around the neck. |
| **moe** | weft strands |
| **man'u** | strand |
| **po'o lau** | butt end of the leaf, or the leaf base that was attached to the hala tree |
| **puhala** | body of a hala tree |
| **ulana** | to plait or weave |

## Weaving Terms:

| | |
|---|---|
| **element** | One single strand used in weaving. |
| **embellishment** | A decorative element inserted into the finished weave. |
| **fold** | A 180-degree bend in an element which is perpendicular to the axis of the element. |
| **prepared lauhala** | Hala leaf that has been soaked and then stretched over the back of a table knife or the sharp edge of a table, six to ten times to make the *lauhala* pliable. |
| **round (kuka'a)** | A coil of prepared *lauhala*—usually 50 leaves or 150 linear feet. The thicker cuticle side of the leaf is the side that is outside the natural curl of the unprepared leaf. When *lauhala* is properly packed into a round, the thicker cuticle side is to the inside of the round. |
| **strand** | A single component or basic unit of the woven fabric. |
| **twill** | A pattern of weaving where each successive row, which is identical to the previous row, steps one warp element to the left or to the right. The resulting pattern has a stair-step effect. |
| **warp** | In horizontal/vertical weaving, the warp elements are the grid through which the weft elements are woven. |
| **weave** | The action of passing the weft over and under the warp. |
| **weaver** | The element that does the action of weaving. Another name for an individual weft element. |
| **weft** | The weaving elements that pass over and under the warp elements. |

## Lauhala Alternatives

**TIP:** *Always prepare, strip and weave lauhala from the po'o lau (base) to the huehuelo (tip). Prepare the koana with great care so that the edges are parallel, and do not cross the veins in the leaf.*

# What if I live in a place that doesn't have *lauhala*? What can I use instead?

**Materials that can be substituted for the bracelet foundation:**

Wooden, plastic, coconut, or metal bracelets with smooth edges. A plastic milk bottle can be cut into long strips and held together with masking tape to make a continuous ring. Flat basket reed, flat oval basket reed, ash splints, hickory bark, etc. can be formed into a continuous ring as well.

**Materials that can be substituted for the wrapping or weaving:**

**Natural fibers:** *Watsonia leaves, bearded iris leaves, rattan peel (cane), split aerial roots, dracena leaves, split philodendron sheaths, palm bark, banana bark, water hyacinth leaves, birch bark, cedar bark, elm bark, split willow, Carex sp, Scirpus sp, bear grass, raffia*

**Manmade Fibers:** *boondoggle (lanyard) lacing, ribbon, yarn, plastic strapping tape used to secure large boxes, cold press watercolor paper*

## Dyeing Lauhala

It is not common to find naturally different colors of dried *lauhala.* Different species of trees will have lighter or darker, redder or browner leaves. Geography can also play a role in determining the color of the leaves.

Picking fresh *lauhala* and then washing and drying it in the sun will produce very light colored, even white, *lauhala.*

Today, many *lauhala* weavers will use natural and commercial dyes to give contrasting colors to their weaving. A simple dye available in most grocery and drug stores as well as fabric and craft shops is Rit™ dye. Available in a large palette of colors, this dye is easy to use and really penetrates the leaf. I use 1/2 bottle (2 oz.) of liquid dye mixed with 1 gallon of hot water and 1 cup of salt. Our favorite colors are Dark Red, Dark Green, Dark Brown, and Black. Dye colors can also be mixed—the Dark Red and Dark Brown make a beautiful red.

**WHAT YOU'LL NEED:**

- a cooking stove
- hot glove mitts
- rubber gloves
- apron or old clothes
- old towels or rags to clean up drips and spills
- 4-oz. bottle of liquid Rit™ dye
- 2 cups of table salt
- pot capable of holding 2 gallons of water – Do not use for cooking food after using it for dyeing.
- a dozen hala leaves, cleaned and prepared
- stick or spoon for stirring

**DIRECTIONS:**

Choose a location to work where you can, not only simmer the leaves in the dye solution, but also transport and hang the dyed leaves, where their drips will not stain or harm anything. Put on your rubber gloves and have discarded towels nearby for spill wipes. Put newspaper on floor and on counters around the stove.

1. Soak the hala leaves in hot water for 20 minutes to pre-moisten them.
2. Bring 1 gallon of water to a boil; turn down the heat so that the water continues to simmer.
3. Add 1 cup of salt and stir.
4. Add 1/2 bottle (2 oz.) of liquid dye and stir—or 1 oz. each of two colors if you want to mix colors.
5. Add the pre-moistened leaves to the dye bath and stir.
6. Simmer the leaves in the dye bath for an hour—frequently checking that the water is only at a simmer and stir the leaves carefully, making sure they remain submerged.
7. When the cuticle side of the leaf is thoroughly dyed, remove the leaves from the dye bath and hang them where they can drip-dry and not stain anything. The color will lighten as it dries so dye the leaves darker than you want them.
8. Put the dyed strips in big roasting pan and take outside to hang on the line or lay on the grass, turning occasionally.
9. Allow the leaves to hang dry for 24 hours to let the dye set.
10. After they have set for 24 hours, rinse the leaves in cold water until the water runs clear.
11. Allow the leaves to dry completely and then roll them into rounds, with the cuticle side in, for storage. (Rolled wet leaves will quickly mildew and rot and be useless.)

# Acknowledgments

On our first trip to Kaua'i my wife and I met an enchanting woman, Amber Ancheta, who introduced us to the world of Hawaiian crafts. Amber's sister, Jolynn Babauta, wove the most beautiful *lauhala* bracelets and inspired us to want to learn how to weave them. I would like to thank Donna Cockett, Corinne Avra, and Jassu Singh for being such talented and cooperative hand models. Lynn Tyrell provided me photographs and information about *lauhala* preparation in Fiji. Jennie Hutchings gave me much appreciated text comments. The *lauhala* strippers made by Deborah-Martinez Rambeau's uncle inspired me to develop the child-friendly *lauhala* strippers for this book. The Kauai Sands Hotel allowed me the use of a conference room as a photo studio for part of this project. Finally, this book could not have been possible without the loving support of my wife, Sher, and son, Andy, and their willingness to take up the slack and follow the paths to which my indulgence led us.


# Bibliography


Bird, Adren. *The Craft of Hawaiian Lauhala Weaving.* Honolulu: University of Hawaii Press, 1982.

Buck, Peter. *Arts and Crafts of Hawaii.* Honolulu: Bishop Museum Press, 1964.

Meilleur, Brien A., MaryAnne B. Maigret, and Richard Manshardt. *Hala and Wauke in Hawaii.* Honolulu: Bishop Museum Press, 1997.

Brigham, William T. *Mat and Basket Weaving of the Ancient Hawaiians Described and Compared with the Basketry of the Other Pacific islanders with an Account of Hawaiian Nets and Nettings by John F. G. Stokes.* Honolulu: Bishop Museum Press, 1906.

Ching, Krohn, Val. *Hawaii Dye Plants and Dye Recipes.* Honolulu: Krohn, 1978.

Cole, Shari, and Vitolia Kulatea. *Cultural Crafts of Niue Pandanus Weaving.* Suva, Fiji: University of the South Pacific, 1996.

Dodge, Ernest. *Hawaiian and other Polynesian Gourds.* Honolulu: Topgallant Pub. Co., 1978.

Kuchler, Susanne, and Graeme Were. *Pacific Patterns.* London: Thames and Hudson, 2005.

Mulford, Judy. *Decorative Marshallese Baskets.* Los Angeles: Wonder Publications, 1991.

Pendergrast, Mick. *Fun with Flax.* Auckland: Reed Methuen, 1987.

Stall, Edna Williamson. *The Story of Lauhala: Leaf of the Pandanus Tree.* Hilo: Petroglyph Press, 1974.


# About the Author

PHOTO: LINDA NOBLITT

**Jim Widess** has owned The Caning Shop in Berkeley, California, since 1971. He is co-author and photographer of *The Caner's Handbook, The Complete Book of Gourd Craft, Making Gourd Musical Instruments, Making Hawaiian Ribbon Leis* (Mutual Publishing), *Complete Book of Gourd Carving, Gourd Dolls and Spirit Figures, Plaited Basketry with Birch Bark* and *Gourds and Fiber* (2011). He is also author and photographer of *Making Hawaiian Musical Instruments, Weaving Hawaiian Coconut Palm Fronds* (Mutual Publishing), *Gourd Pyrography* and *The Complete Guide to Chair Caning.* Jim has a zeal for visual instructions for crafts.


Questions for the author may be sent to jimwidess@caning.com.

## How to Make Hawaiian Ribbon Leis

BY COREEN MIKIOI IWAMOTO AND JIM WIDESS

Leis are symbols of love and friendship, to be given to others with a warm embrace and a kiss. Unlike flower leis, which eventually wither and fade, ribbon leis are treasured throughout the years; they are gifts of aloha that can last a lifetime. For this reason, beautiful and everlasting ribbon leis are a popular alternative to flower leis in the islands as well as on the mainland. With this first-ever easy-to-follow visual guide you can fashion your own ribbon leis from materials found at any craft or fabric store.

Fifteen different ribbon lei designs are showcased – all created to resemble local floral favorites such as pikake, 'ilima, hinahina, firecracker and white ginger.

ISBN-10: 1-56647-575-9
ISBN-13: 978-1-56647-575-4
80 PAGES
FULL COLOR, SOFT COVER
**$14.95**

## How to Make Hawaiian Musical Instruments

BY JIM WIDESS

Hawai'i has a rich musical heritage that is carried on in the rhythmic beat of the ipu and resonant pounding of pahu drums at hula performances throughout the Islands. While many of the musical instruments that accompany hula today can be traced back to early Polynesian roots, others—like the ipu heke gourd drum, ipu hokiokio gourd nose flute and uliuli rattle—are considered to be uniquely Hawaiian, found nowhere else in the world.

Now, for the first time, the manufacturing processes of eighteen traditional Hawaiian musical instruments are documented with carefully researched instructions and step-by-step color photographs in an easy-to-follow craft guide.

ISBN-10: 1-56647-564-3
ISBN-13: 978-1-56647-564-8
80 PAGES
FULL COLOR, SOFT COVER
**$19.95**

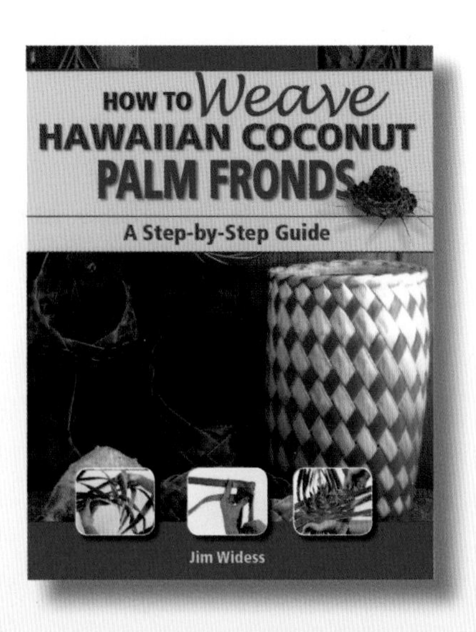


## How to Weave Hawaiian Coconut Palm Fronds

BY JIM WIDESS

The gently swaying coconut palm is certainly a symbol of Hawai'i. Its luscious, long green flexible fronds just tempt you to weave them. Here you'll learn the secrets for palm frond weaving including their preparation and the importance of "racking" the frond. A beautifully laid out book with hundreds of large, detailed, color photographs and clear, written instructions for 11 different projects.

All the critical steps are shown, leaving out nothing. Projects include a round basket, a square basket, a traditional palm frond hat, a trio of hanging baskets, a bird, two fish, a grasshopper, and a rose. Spiral binding allows the book to lay flat.

ISBN-10: 1-56647-797-2
ISBN-13: 978-1-56647-797-0
72 PAGES
FULL COLOR, SOFT COVER
**$18.95**